Color by Fox

W.E.B. Du Bois Institute

Series Editors

Henry Louis Gates, Jr.
W.E.B. Du Bois Professor of Humanities
Harvard University

Richard Newman
Research Officer
The W.E.B. Du Bois Institute
Harvard University

The Open Sore of a Continent
A Personal Narrative of the Nigerian Crisis
Wole Soyinka

From Emerson to King
Democracy, Race and the Politics of Protest
Anita Haya Patterson

Primitivist Modernism
Black Culture and the Origins of Transatlantic Modernism
Sieglinde Lemke

The Burden of Memory, the Muse of Forgiveness
Wole Soyinka

Color by Fox
The Fox Network and the Revolution in Black Television
Kristal Brent Zook

The W.E.B. Du Bois Institute brings together leading scholars from around the world to explore a range of topics in the study of African and African American culture, literature, and history. The Institute series provides a publishing forum for outstanding work deriving from colloquia, research groups, and conferences sponsored by the Institute. Whether undertaken by individuals or collaborative groups, the books appearing in this series work to foster a stronger sense of national and international community and a better understanding of diasporic history.

Color by Fox

The Fox Network and the Revolution in Black Television

Kristal Brent Zook

New York Oxford
OXFORD UNIVERSITY PRESS
1999

Oxford University Press

Oxford New York
Athens Auckland Bangkok Bogotá Buenos Aires Calcutta Cape Town
Chennai Dar es Salaam Delhi Florence Hong Kong Istanbul Karachi
Kuala Lumpur Madrid Melbourne Mexico City Mumbai Nairobi
Paris São Paulo Singapore Taipei Tokyo Toronto Warsaw

and associated companies in
Berlin Ibadan

Published by Oxford University Press, Inc.
198 Madison Avenue, New York, New York 10016

Library of Congress Cataloging-in-Publication Data
Zook, Kristal Brent.
Color by Fox : the Fox network and the revolution in black television / Kristal Brent Zook.
p. cm. — (W.E.B. Du Bois Institute)
Includes bibliographical references and index.
ISBN 0-19-510548-6 — ISBN 0-19-510612-1 (pbk.)
1. Afro-Americans in television. 2. Afro-Americans in television broadcasting. I. Title. II. Series.
PN1992.8.A34 Z66 1999
791.45'6520396073—dc21 98-7853

9 8 7 6 5 4 3 2 1

Printed in the United States of America
on acid-free paper

Contents

Acknowledgments

Since this project began as a doctoral dissertation, I need to go back to my alma mater, the University of California, Santa Cruz, to begin the process of giving thanks. I remain extremely grateful to the devoted network of advisors who read and encouraged early incarnations of this work while I was enrolled in the History of Consciousness Program.

The chair of my dissertation committee, the groundbreaking film theorist Teresa de Lauretis, was especially committed to seeing me finish. Her unshakable confidence in my abilities enabled me to reach beyond what I assumed to be my greatest potential, and for that she has my sincere gratitude.

The brilliant sociologist and television theorist Herman Gray read and critiqued my chapters with the eye of a hawk. He was also my only real role model for doing this type of work and his own provocative writings on black television offered constant inspiration.

The legendary scholar and activist Angela Davis was an indispensable member of my committee as well. Her critical insight provided a much-needed historical perspective, as she reminded me of various modes of cultural resistance within black communities. To work with her was a privilege beyond words.

Although they did not sit on my dissertation committee, I am also indebted to Donna Haraway and James Clifford, who served at various stages in my graduate career as sounding boards and informal advisors. Many thanks also to the Reverend Jesse Jackson, for his guidance and friendship. Perhaps most of all, I am grateful to Professor Elliott Butler-Evans, my chief mentor at the University of California, Santa Barbara. Without his prodding—which was anything but tender—I never would have imagined myself completing a Ph.D.

Having finished the dissertation and established myself as a journalist, it was understandable that this project would migrate from the realm of academia to a popular readership. The final incarnation of this work has therefore been shaped by over a decade of conversations with television executives, writers, producers, directors, and stars. While I am grateful to everyone who provided interviews, I am especially thankful to members of the entertainment community who went beyond the microcassette recorder to share off-the-record insights, encouragement, and friendship. An incomplete list of these includes Nelson George, who was there long before the seed was planted; Warrington Hudlin, my tireless champion; Keenen Ivory Wayans, who exposed me to the other side of producing; and Sinbad.

Thanks also to my extraordinary community of editors for helping me plow through many of the ideas that appear in this book: Manohla Dargis, Elizabeth Pincus, and especially Judith Lewis, at the *LA Weekly;* Lisa Kennedy, of the *Village Voice* and *US* magazine; Carter Harris, at *Vibe;* and my former student, Tracii McGregor, at *The Source* (you've come a long way, baby).

For supporting me in my first "real" teaching job at the University of California, Los Angeles, I thank Valerie Smith and Richard Yarborough. And for inviting me to teach in the land down under, I thank all the wonderful faculty and staff of Murdoch University, in particular Toby Miller, Tom O'Regan, and Irma Whitford. Thanks also to my Aussie friends for welcoming me into their lives and hearts: Len and Lisa Collard, Linda and Alec Pismiris, Geoff and Jody Beaty, Denise Groves, and especially my sweetheart, Damien Jeffrey Weber.

I also want to thank my circle back home, a support network that spans the decades from high school to the present: David Valdez, my soulmate and brother; Karen Williams, who knew me even before we met; Monique and Rena Braud, for making sure I didn't forget to laugh; Traci Lynn Blackwell; Donna Franklin; Trey and Erika Ellis; and Lee Kyle Gaither.

The process of securing photo permissions was a living hell until Alfred Bie of Fox Publicity came along. I thank both Alfred and Kevin Fitzgerald for caring enough to make it happen. I also thank megascholar Henry Louis Gates Jr., without whom this project would not have landed so happily at Oxford University Press, and my editor at Oxford, T. Susan Chang, for her level-headedness and calm.

Finally, I offer this book as a testament to the strength and endurance of my family. Being able to finish college is an honor that I do not take lightly. Without the love and support of those who nurtured me from girlhood to writer, life's hurdles would have seemed insurmountable. I thank my mother, Beverly Guenin, for instilling a love of words in me from the time I was in her womb; my grandmother, Christine Brent, for supporting my every goal with the tenacity of an Olympic coach; my sister-cousin, Lisa Brent, who listened to and applauded the pages of this book more than anyone else; my aunt and uncle, Mary Katherine and Arthur Brent, for offering a safe shelter when I needed it most; and my father, Phillip Zook, whose solid presence in my life today was worth the wait. This book is dedicated to all of you.

Los Angeles
January 1998

Color by Fox

Introduction

I began this project ten years ago. It was a time when most anyone with a bit of melanin (and some without) found themselves caught up in a rising tide of neonationalism—the era of early Spike Lee films, Public Enemy's "Fight the Power," and other such revolutionary expressive forms. It seemed that everyone wanted to be black—at least in theory, if not in practice. Just as an Afro had defined "downness" in the social parlance of the 1960s and 70s, so too did a red, black, and green Africa medallion or a "40 Acres and a Mule" T-shirt now signify racial authenticity.[1]

I was a twenty-two-year-old, self-consciously light-skinned graduate student, and I too wanted to be "really black" (as opposed to, as one dreadlocked professor referred to me, "not really black"). While at the time I never would have described my overly earnest interviews with rappers such as KRS-One and filmmakers such as John Singleton as attempts to come to terms with my own ambiguous racial positionality, they were just that.

There were two primary locations, I found, from which we spoke as black Americans. One, a space largely occupied by "boyz in the 'hood" films and rap music, was about the pain of exclusion from mainstream America; it was also about violence and masculinity. The other was about very different kinds of exclusions, different kinds of suffering. This is not to say that such realms did not overlap, of course. But the second realm was more obvious in the world of black television production, as well as in the works of black women writers.

In the fiction of Toni Cade Bambara, Kristin Hunter, Audre Lorde, and Michelle Cliff, for example, creative reconfigurations of "home" worked to recuperate blackness from always meaning "heterosexual," "male," "poor," and "criminal." Sometimes, argued these authors, blackness was also about being a feminist, being light-skinned, being privileged, and/or loving women. Blackness, in other words, was also about the complex processes of acculturation and *intra*racial estrangement.

At about the same time that black women novelists were enjoying heightened interest in their work, an emergent genre of black-produced television (which I locate both during and after the success of *The Cosby Show*) also highlighted intraracial differences. In the late 1980s and early 90s, shows such as *Cosby, A Different World,* and *The Fresh Prince of Bel Air* presented the refreshing possibility that racial authenticity could be negotiated rather than assumed—or perhaps even done away with altogether.

What emerged were contested narratives that challenged the very notion of "blackness" itself. Despite a seemingly coherent nationalist aesthetic (like kente decor, black-owned co-ops and cafés, historically black universities), these narratives were about more than a seamless Afrocentricism. Rather, they wrestled with the unspoken pleasures (and horrors) of assimilation, the shock of integration, and the pain of cultural homelessness.

Given the social and economic context of the time, it was understandable that such contradictory representations would appear. With the "success" of integration and affirmative action in the 1960s and 70s, unusually large numbers of African Americans had been granted economic mobility. More privileged than any generation before them, this "buffer" caste, although only a small fraction of the total African American population, experienced a certain, strange inclusion, one that blurred established notions of race. Unlike the 1960s and before, who "counted" as black was no longer clear by the 1980s. Nor was it clear who now suffered enough to be a "legitimate" family member.

Successful African American producers, directors, writers, and entertainers (as well as viewers) also wrestled with these questions. Black productions of the 1990s were individual autobiographies as well as communal outpourings of group desire—collective rememberings not unlike slave narratives. During this period, black producers and consumers engaged in awkward modes of resistance and representation. It seemed that we wanted both capitalism and communalism; feminism as well as a singular, authentic self; patriarchy plus liberation; Africa the motherland *and* the American dream. These yearnings were explored, celebrated, and contested in black-produced shows of the 90s.

Because most of the productions discussed in this book aired on the Fox network (the bulk of this project having been completed prior to the debut of copycats Warner Brothers and United Paramount), I begin with a brief history of the fourth network and the structural shifts that enabled its ascent.[2]

In the 1980s middle-class white audiences began to replace standard network viewing with cable subscriptions and videocassette recorders. Since working-class African American and Latino audiences in general did not yet have access to these new technologies, they continued to rely on the "free" networks—NBC, CBS, and ABC. Consequently, "urban" audiences suddenly became a key demographic in the overall network viewership. During this period, black audiences watched 44 percent more network television than nonblacks. What's more, they clearly preferred black shows.[3]

These shifts had a profound effect on television programming. In the mid-1980s good pitches, or show ideas presented to producers, began to be defined as those appealing to both "urban" and "mainstream" audiences. NBC, in particular, boasted crossover hits such as *The Cosby Show* (the nation's number one program for five seasons), *A Different World*, and *The Fresh Prince of Bel Air*. In fact, NBC could even be considered something of a prototype for Fox's urban network, given that it had always carried more "ethnic" shows than either CBS or ABC.[4] (When Fox owner Rupert Murdoch assembled his programming department, he even brought Garth Ancier, Kevin Wendle, and other former NBC employees on board.)

The new network launched in 1986. By "narrowcasting" or targeting a specific black viewership (what Pam Veasey referred to cynically as the "Nike and Doritos audience"), and "counter-programming" against other shows to suit that audience's taste, Fox was able to capture large numbers of young, urban viewers. By 1993, the fourth network was airing the largest single crop of black-produced shows in television history. And by 1995 black Americans (some 12 percent of the total U.S. population) were a striking 25 percent of Fox's market.

The Fox network was unique, then, in that it inadvertently fostered a space for black authorship in television. It did this to capitalize on an underrepresented market, of course. But the fact that entertainers such as Keenen Ivory Wayans, Charles Dutton, Martin Lawrence, and Sinbad were made executive producers of their own shows was no small feat. Such titles increased (to varying degrees) their decision-making power and enabled them to hire writers, producers, and directors who shared their visions.

After Keenan Ivory Wayans's 1988 $3 million film *I'm Gonna Git You Sucka* made $20 million at the box office, the director-comedian held a private screening for Fox film executives, hoping to get financial backing and distribution for his next project. Although no film executives showed up at the screening, Fox's TV people did, offering Wayans a weekly half-hour series in which he could do "whatever he wanted." So it was that Wayans became the creator, director, executive producer, and star of *In Living Color,* an unprecedented arrangement for a black entertainer in 1990.

Fox was "completely different" from traditional networks in its early days, recalled Wayans.[5] "Barry Diller, who had been responsible for bringing Eddie Murphy to Paramount, was there. And there were a lot of other young, cutting-edge executives.

They wanted to be the rebel network." In fact, had Wayans's idea for a sketch variety show like *In Living Color* come along in the 1980s, noted Twentieth Television president Harris Katleman, it would have been considered "too ethnic." Fox aired the irreverent series when it did because it needed "an intriguing spin" to distinguish it from the more traditional networks.[6]

It was in this same spirit that Fox programmer Garth Ancier had approached the comedy writing team of Ron Leavitt and Michael Moye (who are white and black, respectively) three years earlier. "Do anything you want," said Ancier, "but make sure it's different. . . . Fox is here to give you the chance to do things you can't do anywhere else."[7] While Leavitt and Moye had written for shows like *The Jeffersons* in the past, it was extremely rare, in 1987, for a black writer to create his (and certainly never her) own series. *Married . . . with Children,* Leavitt and Moye's invention, went on to become the longest-running sitcom in network history.

We should look more closely, then, at what I see as four key elements of black-produced television. Based on over a decade of researching shows that have black casts and involve a significant degree of black creative control, I have found that four common traits reappear consistently. These can be summarized as: autobiography, meaning a tendancy toward collective and individual authorship of black experience; improvisation, the practice of inventing and ad-libbing unscripted dialogue or action; aesthetics, a certain pride in visual signifiers of blackness; and drama, a marked desire for complex characterizations and emotionally challenging subject matter. Throughout this book, I refer to these four traits as a way of recognizing and identifying common ideological trends within black productions.

In addition to these common traits, black shows may also be identified thematically, as most have a tendency to revisit issues of deep significance to in-group audiences. (By "in-group" or "in-house," I refer to audience members who are not necessarily black, but who identify with what may be described as shared "black" positionalities, experiences, memories, or desires.) This book is organized in three sections to reflect such thematic overlappings. It is important to note that some shows which may seem crucial to this discussion—such as ABC's *Family Matters,* the longest-running black sitcom of all time—are deliberately left out. This is because such shows are more accurately categorized as mainstream programs with black casts, than as complex black productions containing the dynamic qualities described above.

Having said that, Part 1 looks at color and caste in *The Fresh Prince of Bel Air, The Sinbad Show, South Central,* and *Pearl's Place to Play*. Part 2 highlights questions of gender and sexuality through readings of *Martin* and *Living Single.* Part 3 explores representations of political movement in both *Roc* and *New York Undercover.* It should be noted that these are by no means neat divisions. On the contrary, every show mentioned in this book is read *in dialogue with* the others. *New York Undercover,* as we shall see, is as concerned with issues of color, beauty, and sexuality as *Martin* and *Living Single* are with class mobility. Nevertheless, such thematic categorizations are helpful, I think, for our purposes here.

Beginning with the first trait of black television, then, we should know that to talk about autobiography, or authorship, in television is tricky, given that there can never be a single "author" of any particular show. As Tim Reid put it, there's "always somebody else you've got to answer to in network television . . . There's this guy and this guy's boss. Then that division and that division's boss. Then the network. Then the advertisers. They're like lawyers," said Reid. "They stand in front of you five and six deep, and they all have a say in the quality of what you're doing." In short, television production is a collective process, and black television in particular reveals group memories as well as individual ones.

For example, writer-producer Rob Edwards *(A Different World)* notes that he has often run "into trouble" by making in-group references while working on white shows. "I would start pitching stuff from a specifically black childhood," he recalls. "Like parents combing your hair. [But] you can't pitch a nap joke on *Full House.*"[8] Writer-producer Susan Fales *(A Different World)* agrees.

"There's a certain gift of the gab . . . a tendency to riff," she notes, "that has been a part of our survival and is absolutely more common on black-produced shows." This penchant for improvisation, says Fales, "can also lead to problems . . . like when actors refer to 'ashy skin.' You can't do that unless you're a very big hit."

Not only are black-produced scripts full of such collective autobiographical references, but these allusions also appear, as Fales indicates, in unscripted forms such as slips of the tongue, bloopers, and ad-libbed dialogue. This leads us to the second characteristic of black television: improvisation.

Historically, the improvisational practices of "cuttin' up" and "playing the dozens" have enabled black Americans to communicate with one another, often under hostile conditions. As Henry Louis Gates, Jr. suggests (borrowing from Claudia Mitchell-Kernan), the Signifying Monkey is able to signify—a rhetorical strategy of resistance characterized by "marking, loud-talking, testifying, calling out (of one's name), sounding, rapping, playing the dozens"—because "the Lion does not understand the nature of the monkey's discourse. . . . The monkey speaks figuratively, in a symbolic code; the lion interprets or reads literally and suffers the consequences of his folly, which is a reversal of his status as King of the Jungle."[9] Cultural theorists have also described this private discourse as "bivocality," "in-jokes," and "minor discourse."[10] Whatever we may call it, such in-group referencing is certainly a dialogic process in black television.

During a taping of Fox's *The Show*, for example, the predominantly African American and Latino studio audience failed to respond when comedian Mystro Clark followed his script closely in a scene with white co-star Sam Seder. In scenes with other black actors however, Clark spontaneously broke into improvisation, which the audience loved. From that point on, network executives routinely instructed black performers on the series to "play the dozens" during tapings.

Autobiography and collective memory are also revealed

"extratextually," or outside a given narrative. While I have discussed briefly how autobiography and collective memory appear in the narratives of TV show scripts and unscripted dialogue, David Marc argues that television personalities relate to audiences in three ways: through a "frankly fictional" character; through a "presentational" character, in which the actor appears as her- or himself within a theatrical space such as a commercial; and through a "documentary" persona, in which the actor's real-life activities, opinions, and lifestyle are revealed through outside media.[11] Viewers register presentational and documentary associations linked to an actor as well as the fictional character he or she plays. (One may think of how this assemblage works in the case of someone like Bill Cosby, whose fictional Cliff Huxtable of *The Cosby Show* combines with the presentational image of the wholesome spokesperson for Jell-O pudding and the documentary persona of the real-life family man and philanthropist found in Cosby's autobiographical best-seller *Fatherhood.*)[12] Often, it is by examining fictional, presentational, and documentary personas together that we begin to recognize the most dynamic and intriguing patterns in our own reception practices.

The third characteristic of black television is culturally specific aesthetics. While rap music and graffiti-like graphics were common on white shows of this era as well, Afrocentric clothing, hair styles, and artifacts performed specific functions in black shows. Frequent references to Malcolm X in *The Fresh Prince of Bel Air, Martin,* and *Roc,* for instance, in the form of posters, photographs, and T-shirts, invoked romanticized spaces of mythical unity and nationalist desire.[13]

Characters on *A Different World* displayed images of Yannick Noah, a world-renowned black French tennis player, and Angela Davis on their dormitory walls. Sportswear carrying the names of black colleges such as Howard and Spelman were common sights on *The Cosby Show, A Different World, Roc, The Sinbad Show,* and *Living Single,* as were black-owned publications like *Emerge, Ebony,* and *Essence.* The paintings of Varnette Honeywood featured in the Huxtable home even led some viewers and producers to invest in her work.[14]

Like the 1960s' *The Bill Cosby Show,* which included frequent references to H. Rap Brown, dashikis, and soul food, such aesthetic markings did more than construct imagined community: They proposed a politics.[15] In his highly successful sitcom of the 1980s, Cosby even went to battle with NBC (and won) over an "Abolish Apartheid" sticker on Theo Huxtable's bedroom door.[16]

The fourth trait of black television is the struggle for drama. Whereas traditional sitcom formats demanded a "joke per page," many black productions of the 1980s and 90s resisted such norms by consciously and unconsciously crafting dramatic episodes. With less explicit story lines, unresolved endings, and increasingly complex characters, these "dramedies" allowed for exploration of painful in-group memories and experiences.[17]

While dramedies were often praised on white sitcoms (for example, in *Home Improvement*'s treatment of leukemia), such moves on black shows were rarely welcomed by networks, as was made clear with the cancellation of *Frank's Place,* a hard-hitting dramedy that looked at intraracial class and color differences among other issues. "There have been sparks of renewed hope in television," noted Tim Reid, who starred in and produced the show. "[But] the attempt to redefine the black sitcom formula is still a goal."[18]

Another example of network resistance to black drama was NBC's premature cancellation of *A Different World.* In its first season, the show was set in "a black college with a lot of white faces," said former staff writer Calvin Brown Jr. (Viewers may recall Marisa Tomei's early appearances.) "Although they had Thad Mumford and Susan Fales," said Brown, "the first season was not black-produced." That changed by season three, however, when Bill Cosby hired director-producer Debbie Allen to revamp the series.

Because Allen encouraged her largely African American staff to explore serious issues, the sitcom began to evolve around dramatic story lines: a woman physically abused by her boyfriend, a student with AIDS, white racism toward black shoppers in a posh jewelry store. One episode even addressed intraracial color prejudice and the fact that some light-skinned southerners had owned slaves. As Susan Fales recalled, this was a particularly explosive episode. "Discussion went on for three hours after that first table reading," said Fales. "The actors and writers had such painful memories . . . and we got so many calls and letters. People connected with the show on a very profound level."

"Debbie Allen came on and saved us," recalled former cast member Sinbad, as the show became, in the words of J. Fred MacDonald, "a vehicle for exploring social problems as disparate as date rape and the high percentage of blacks in the U.S. military."[19] But while *A Different World* remained among the top five of all shows according to Nielsen (and even, at one point, outranked *Cosby* among black viewers in particular), the series was oddly canceled in 1991.

"Advertisers started requesting scripts of the show beforehand," recalled Debbie Allen. "This was new. But I had been given orders by Bill Cosby himself to go in and clean house, and to make it a show about intelligent young black people." Indeed, Allen had been given a rare opportunity; one that would not come again anytime soon. Although Allen continued to direct sitcoms such as *The Sinbad Show,* and later starred in NBC's *In the House,* she recognized that even black productions (such as the latter, created by Winifred Hervey Stallworth and produced by Quincy Jones) were not necessarily going to be "issue-oriented." "Like the buffoons in Shakespeare," concluded Susan Fales, "we were not regarded as interesting enough for drama."

Three years later the Fox network also canceled *The Sinbad Show, Roc, South Central* and *In Living Color*—four of its six black productions—in one fell swoop. Reverend Jesse Jackson initiated boycott threats and letter-writing campaigns; Ralph Farquhar and Tina Lifford (producer and star of *South Central,* respectively) traveled to Washington, D.C., to enlist the support of the Congressional Black Caucus; and Representative Ed Towns (D-NY) lambasted what he called the network's "plantation programming." "Fox-TV created its niche based upon racy, black, and youth-oriented programming," said a press release from the congressman's office. "Apparently, as the network moves to become more mainstream, its attitude to positive black programs is, we don't need, nor want them anymore. . . . I can assure you, the CBC [Congressional Black Caucus] and the black community is not going to allow [Rupert Murdoch] to blatantly treat us with disrespect and apparent contempt."

And yet it did. Fox cited poor ratings in canceling the shows, but it wasn't black faces or producers that did the programs in: It was black *complexity*. After Murdoch spent $1.6 billion on the rights to the National Football League's Sunday games, the network began to seek white "legitimacy." As Calvin Brown Jr. explained, only black folks and teenagers were watching Fox in its early days, "so they could get away with a little more. But now with football, baseball, and hockey, that's over. We won't ever have another space in network television like that again."[20]

The spaces "won" for difference in popular culture are carefully policed and regulated, writes cultural theorist Stuart Hall. True, but stay tuned. What happened in black television in the early 90s went beyond the policeable.

Part 1

Color and Caste

Then Gold spoke up and said, "Now, lemme tell one. Ah know one about a man as black as Gene."

"Whut you always crackin' me for?" Gene wanted to know. "Ah ain't a bit blacker than you."

"Oh, yes you is, Gene. Youse a whole heap blacker than Ah is."

"Aw, go head on, Gold. Youse blacker than me. You jus' look my color cause youse fat. If you wasn't no fatter than me you'd be so black till lightnin' bugs would follow you at twelve o'clock in de day, thinkin' it's midnight."

"Dat's a lie, youse blacker than Ah ever dared to be. Youse lam' black. Youse so black till they have to throw a sheet over y' head so de sun kin rise every mornin'. Ah know yo' ma cried when she seen you."

From Mules and Men,
by Zora Neale Hurston, 1939

1

Blood Is Thicker than Mud: C-Note Goes to Compton on The Fresh Prince of Bel Air

In the 1980s much was made of the *The Cosby Show*'s challenge to black "authenticity." With its doctor-lawyer parents and college-bound kids, *Cosby* was a controversial attempt to uncouple blackness and poverty. But what most cultural theorists failed to note was the ongoing nature of this representational struggle, which reached new heights with the 1990 debut of *The Fresh Prince of Bel Air.*

Although sold as a lighthearted, "fish-out-of-water" tale (a combination of *The Beverly Hillbillies* and *Diff'rent Strokes*), the ideological tensions underlying this sitcom were far from frivolous. Rather, *The Fresh Prince of Bel Air* was a collective autobiographical narrative about the traumas of integration in a post–civil-rights era. Not only did it take the black upper class for granted, as had *Cosby,* but it also wrestled, frequently and openly, with economic and cultural mobility.

The show's premise revolved around an inner-city teen who was forced to relocate to the wealthy, predominately white community of Bel Air, California. The opening credit sequence sets the stage, as actor Will Smith (the real-life rapper formerly known as the "Fresh Prince") is shown on a basketball court in his "rough" Philadelphia neighborhood. When his character, also called Will, accidentally hits a local hoodlum with the basketball, there is a comic allusion to violence, followed by a quick flight out to California. As the show's theme song goes: "This is a story all about how my life turned twisted upside down / I got in one little fight and my mom got scared / She said, 'You're moving [in] with your auntie and uncle in Bel Air.'"[1]

Upon arrival at the lavish home of his aunt and uncle, Vivian and Philip Banks (Vivian was played by both Janet Hubert-Whitten and Daphne Maxwell Reid; James Avery was Philip), Will also finds his three upper-crust cousins: Hilary (Karyn Parsons), a self-absorbed shopaholic; Carlton (Alfonso Ribeiro), the family nerd; and young Ashley (Tatyana M. Ali), whom Will eventually teaches to rap and dance. Rounding out the cast is Geoffrey (Joseph Marcell), the family's British-accented butler.

Based on the real-life experiences of show producer Benny Medina, *The Fresh Prince* is a clear example of collective autobiography. Like Will Smith's character, Medina also found himself on the edge of lawlessness during his teenage years. In and out of foster homes and detention centers throughout Watts and south Los Angeles, Medina was eventually taken in by a wealthy Westside couple: television composer Jack Elliott and his wife, Bobbi Elliott. At Beverly Hills High, Medina befriended the sons of then Motown president Berry Gordy, and eventually went on to become a Warner Brothers music executive himself.

Medina first discussed the concept for *The Fresh Prince* with Will Smith informally, at a taping of *The Arsenio Hall Show.* Not long after a pitch meeting with music producer Quincy Jones and Kevin Wendle, then president of Quincy Jones Entertainment, Jones put in a call to NBC executive Brandon Tartikoff. Eventually the idea was was given a "green light."

Perhaps Medina's story resonated with Jones because both men had experienced a similar sense of racial and cultural displacement. Born on Chicago's South Side, Jones had also lived in a segregated African American community as a boy before moving to Seattle, Washington. As a young pianist and trumpeter, Jones later won a scholarship to the Berklee College of Music in Boston, where he experienced yet another cultural dislocation. When a heart condition prevented him from pursuing a career as a trumpeter, Jones became vice president of Mercury Records, one of the first black executives to achieve such a rank in a white music corporation. In his personal life, Jones married three times, to three white women, and fathered six biracial children.[2]

I include such intimate details because they're important to understanding the politics of black television. It wasn't long ago, after all, that men like Jones were brutally persecuted for having interracial affairs, fathering half-white babies, or aspiring to own businesses. In fact, both Jones and Medina belonged to a relatively new social formation.

The Fresh Prince revealed the ironies of such shifting caste positionalities. More than once Jones himself expressed concern for what he called "black-on-black prejudice" among "haves and have-nots." It was an issue that Jones, Medina, and Smith all agreed to address on their show. In vowing to examine such intraracial dynamics, they successfully wrestled with collective African American memories and desires. And yet it is important to recall, as J. Fred MacDonald notes, that 93 percent of black shows (apart from *The Cosby Show* and *A Different World*) were still run by white producers in the late 1980s.[3] *The Fresh Prince* was no exception.

Because neither Medina nor Jones had experience running a television series, NBC was not initially willing to entrust them with its investment. Instead, the network brought in Andy and Susan Borowitz, a white, Harvard-educated writing team, to oversee production. As the show proved successful, however, and tensions grew between the Borowitzes and other members of the creative team, NBC agreed to give Medina and Jones more power. By the end of the first season the Borowitzes had resigned under "not-so-friendly circumstances" and were soon replaced by Winifred Hervey Stallworth, a former writer and producer on *The Cosby Show.*

From Benny Medina's perspective, the Borowitzes had been more interested in "jokes" (or what *Esquire* once referred to as their "street shtick," formerly seen on shows such as *Webster*) than believable depictions of black life.[4] Quincy Jones thought their writing "contrived and wrong." And Will Smith confessed to journalists that he often provided behind-the-scenes cultural tutoring for the couple. When the Banks children were to behave disrespectfully, for example, Smith suggested to the Borowitzes that generally speaking black kids, unlike white kids, "absolutely do not . . . raise their voice in the presence of their parents." But as Smith acknowledged, these white writers "didn't quite understand that concept."[5]

Indeed, Susan Borowitz admitted that she listened to rap music for the first time as something of "a homework assignment" for working on the show. The Borowitzes also received "a crash course" from Smith, she said, in hip-hop terms like *fly* and *dope.*[6] After all, as Andy Borowitz later conceded, black sitcom writing is largely "guesswork" done by whites. "You have eight white writers in a room with one black trainee," he explained, "and they ask him: 'Do blacks still say *def* a lot?' "[7]

Of course, collective black autobiography found its way into story lines despite the Borowitzes' leadership, as male characters, in particular, engaged in ongoing struggles to redefine racial authenticity. In the premiere episode, for example, Will is constructed as working-class, boisterous, and uncouth. He is also seen as hip and culturally "authentic." After stapling a Malcolm X poster to his bedroom wall, he shows up for a formal business dinner with a tuxedo cummerbund wrapped across his bare chest, much to the dismay of his uncle, a prestigious attorney who is entertaining business associates.

The episode is intriguing in that it challenges the very notion of black "authenticity"—that is, the myth that one's cultural heritage can be simplistically determined by fashion, income, or lifestyle. While Will is shocked to learn that his bourgeois uncle had been politically active during the 1960s (and had even heard Malcolm X speak in person), Philip Banks is stunned to discover that his "ghettoish" nephew plays classical piano.

Similar revelations occur between Will and Geoffrey, the butler (whose love of opera and fine art construct him as less "black" than Will). The most interesting of these exchanges, however, involve Will's straightlaced cousin, Carlton. In the remainder of this chapter I focus on two episodes: one in which the cousins are pitted against each other, and another in which they defend their shared allegiances and blood ties.

In the first episode, written by Rob Edwards, Will and Jazz (played by Smith's rap partner, Jeff Townes, or "D.J. Jazzy Jeff") overhear Carlton's glee club rehearsing. In one of the series' most clever scenes ever, the prim, all-white quintet delivers—under Carlton's direction—a studied rendition of the Commodores' classic funk jam "Brick House," complete with well-rounded vowels and exaggerated enunciation. "If the Commodores heard you singing that," cracks Will, "they'd tie you down to the tracks and run you over with the Soul Train." From there, the exchange goes straight from a clever banter about soul, funk, and the ability to groove to the heart of the matter: Carlton's lack of blackness.

"Just because I grew up in the best neighborhood and pronounce the *i-n-g*'s at the end of my words doesn't make me any less black than you," quips Carlton. "Naw. It's that tie that does it," retorts Jazz for the punchline. The end result of this toast is a bet: Will and Jazz wager that Carlton can't last two days in Compton, Jazz's neighborhood.

This episode is especially fascinating for its intertextuality; that is, the way it brings together fictional, presentational, and documentary representations. By constructing Will and Jazz as authentic "niggahs," the narrative becomes richly complicated for in-group viewers—particularly for those who realize that

Jazzy Jeff and the Fresh Prince never occupied such a space as rappers. On the contrary, their music was regarded as mainstream pop. Even Susan Borowitz acknowledged that "hardcore" hip-hop fans might resent the show's "cuddly" packaging of rap.[8]

So while references to Compton—with its connotations of gangsta rap and groups like N.W.A. ("Niggahs With Attitude")—work to transfer images of "realness" to Will and Jazz, such images are actually diametrically opposed, if not hostile, to the pop personas of the Fresh Prince and Jazzy Jeff. Taking such intertextual dynamics a step further, the text becomes even more intriguing: Former N.W.A. member Dr. Dre was said to have financed his Death Row Records with profits from Vanilla Ice, the infamous white rapper who claimed to have a criminal record and black family ties in order to appear more "authentic." My point is that the text itself explodes any easy definitions of "real" blackness.

Meanwhile, Carlton surprises Will by not only surviving but thriving in the 'hood. When Will arrives at Jazz's Compton apartment, he expects to find his usual nerdy cousin. Instead he is greeted by "C-Note," who—in a brilliant turn by actor Alfonso Ribeiro—successfully mimics, performs, and constructs "blackness." Whereas Carlton carried himself with straight-A posture, C-Note moves casually, with rounded shoulders and a suddenly broad, muscular back—donning dark sunglasses and a gangsta-like bandanna. Having studied "hip-hop flashcards," he now speaks the language of "the streets."

"Carlton, what's wrong with you?" cries Will. "Yo, Prince," replies C-Note, oddly invoking the rapper's real-life stage name. "How you gonna play me?" The moment is extraordinary, a classic—unfortunately, it is interrupted too soon by Vivian Banks, who has rushed across town to rescue her "baby," Carlton, from the dangers of Compton.

Barging into Jazz's apartment and scolding the boys for not keeping a tidier home, Vivian Banks orders her son to return home. Her insertion here is disappointing in two ways. One, it forecloses the scene's potential for redefining "blackness" by returning Carlton to a "proper" identity (i.e., educated and rich, and therefore not black). And two, it avoids what could have been a rare exploration of acculturation and black femaleness.

Instead, story lines involving Vivian, Hilary, and Ashley generally cling to stereotypically "feminine" concerns, such as shopping, dating, marriage, pregnancy, child rearing, aging, and beauty. In fact, I was unable to find a single episode, in six seasons, in which women characters were central to dramatic confrontations around racial identity, gender, or class.

Quincy Jones may have inadvertently shed light on this gap in a 1995 *Los Angeles Times* interview. "I always worried about my son having first-generation money," he confessed. (Jones is also the father of five daughters.) "I think it's important for a male child to understand what the street's about, because the sensibility of the world is really driven by the street. . . . It's OK for your daughters not to experience that, but for a boy, I think you can set him back by not letting him have that part of his life."[9]

Again, autobiography is crucial here. According to Benny Medina, the character of Hilary is based on a wealthy black Beverly Hills woman he knew as a teenager, a woman who, as Medina recalls, didn't approve of his friendship with her sons. "She didn't marry a doctor and move to Beverly Hills so her children would hang around with little black kids," he noted.[10]

Unfortunately, such constructions of black women trivialize issues of gender, color, and caste. As bell hooks notes in a different context, the implication is that black women are predisposed to a certain mindless acculturation, whereas the men around them somehow manage "to question, reflect upon, and . . . [even] resist such processes."[11] It is especially ironic that women's experiences are so consistently silenced in black television, given that black female viewers outnumber black males by far.[12]

While writer-producers such as Yvette Lee Bowser, Winifred Hervey Stallworth, and Debbie Allen have also used the medium autobiographically, they have only rarely focused on "womanist" issues. The NBC sitcom *In the House,* for example, was created by Stallworth in 1995, following her tenure at *The Fresh Prince.* The show starred Debbie Allen as a middle-aged woman facing divorce, alimony struggles, and the problem of finding employment. Although Stallworth had herself experienced a divorce, her show did not venture into dramatic explorations of class or gender. It seems that this terrain remained reserved for men.

Three years after Carlton's Compton bet, a strikingly similar episode of *The Fresh Prince* aired. It opens on campus at a fictional Los Angeles University, where new students Will and Carlton are seen checking out information booths during fraternity rush week. Predictably, Carlton gravitates toward a table hosted by white members, who greet him with the following: "We're Delta Gamma Nu, our blood is very blue, our money's old, our cards are gold, and who the heck are you?"

Next, black fraternity members enter, performing a traditional "step" routine, complete with rhythmic stomping and clapping. Following rousing applause from the studio audience and cast (even director Chuck Vinson was surprised by the power of this scene), the punch line is delivered by a bewildered Carlton, who returns to the stodgy Delta Gamma Nus and asks: "Can I hear yours again?"

Following a commercial break, however, Carlton and Will agree to rush the black fraternity, Phi Beta Gamma, where the running joke soon becomes Carlton's "white" lifestyle. While Carlton's lack of "blackness" is again under attack in this episode, the site of struggle has shifted. This time, it's Top Dog, the fraternity pledge leader, who challenges Carlton's authenticity, while Will, surprisingly, comes to his cousin's defense.[13]

The pivotal confrontation occurs at the Phi Beta Gamma pledge party, when Will learns that he has been accepted but Carlton has not. As Will and Top Dog face off, their profiles are framed interestingly by director Vinson. Behind them, a dreadlocked, brown-skinned brothah dances in a cool, meditative manner. In contrast, we see Carlton moving with spastic, exaggerated motions.

Against these images Top Dog explains that Carlton's Ralph Lauren shirts, wing-tip shoes, and corporate look do not exemplify what he thinks a Phi Beta Gamma should be. "We don't need a brother like him in this fraternity," he tells Will. (Also in the background, another dreadlocked fraternity member chats with two light-skinned women. Again, female characters are situated primarily as ornamental objects here, rather than complex characters with their own histories and subjectivities. In this scene, female partygoers are almost universally light-skinned and/or with long, blond hair.)

The episode takes its unusual dramatic turn when Carlton learns that he has been dubbed "not enough of a brothah to be a brothah." Suddenly the music stops and all eyes are on him. "But I did everything," he protests. "I cooked, I cleaned, I hand-washed your toilets." "Yeah," replies Top Dog bitterly. "Everything your butler does for you! I'm not accepting no prep-school, Bel Air–bred sell-out into my fraternity."

But Carlton, the man who once studied hip-hop flashcards to prove his "blackness," is not yet ready to give up. "You think I'm a sell-out. Why? Because I live in a big house, or I dress a certain way? . . . Being black isn't what I'm trying to be. It's what I *am.* I'm running the same race and jumping the same hurdles you are, so why are you tripping me up? You said we need to stick together, but you don't even know what that means. If you ask me, *you're* the real sell-out."

Carlton's dramatic speech is followed by energetic applause from audience members, and unlike the 1990 episode in which he is forcibly returned home by his mother, the cousins now retreat of their own accord, returning to the safety of their unified household, as the episode's title tells us, borrowing from Sly and the Family Stone's 1970s hit, "blood is thicker than mud."

Upon hearing of Carlton's rejection, Philip Banks reacts with yet another, unusually dramatic scene. "This really irritates me," he begins, pacing the floor of his living room. "I've worked very hard to give my family a good life, and suddenly somebody tells me there's a penalty for success. . . . When are we gonna stop doing this to each other?" Two dramatic beats are followed by motionless shots of the entire family and finally the credits, rolled in silence.[14]

This episode illustrates clearly the shift in Will and Carlton's relationship and, by extension, in the show's overall ideological stance. As Will moves away from narrow notions of "authenticity," viewers are also encouraged to entertain the possibility that "blackness" is not fixed but fluid.

At the conclusion of the show's first season, following Andy and Susan Borowitz's departure, African American writer and producer Stallworth came on board, vowing that she would make the characters "more real." In the end, however, the series was exactly what NBC hoped it would be: a mass-appeal *comedy* in which Will Smith "charms, disarms, and alarms [viewers] with his streetwise ways."[15] As Mim Udovitch noted in *The Village Voice*, "Everything that made [Smith] seem like a lightweight, middle-class exercise as a rapper [also enjoyed] a favorable exchange rate in the currency of situation comedy."[16] This was a network, after all, that was "quite taken aback" when Smith's character hung an image of Malcolm X on the wall.[17]

Despite increasing degrees of black control and authorship, then, in-group issues were only rarely addressed in a dramatic manner. And yet *The Fresh Prince* provided a striking indication of what was to come. The "freshest" thing about it, noted Medina at the conclusion of the show's run, was that it made explicit the "widening gap between the classes of African Americans."[18] Similar in-group dialogues would later emerge on black productions at Fox. That these shows made it to the air at all represented a veritable revolution for network television.

2
High Yella Bananas and Hair Weaves: The Sinbad Show

Although it lasted only one season (1993–94), *The Sinbad Show* provides a prime illustration of struggles that often take place within black television. Clearly containing the four common elements of black TV—autobiography, improvisation, aesthetics, and drama—the show's behind-the-scenes politics of production offered important insights as to why in-group textual conversations among African Americans so often meet with resistance among predominantly white network executives and advertisers.

Through its collective conversations about color and caste, *The Sinbad Show* expressed the duality and contradiction common to many black productions: that is, it highlighted the need to celebrate "our" shared experience (what I call nationalist desire), while at the same time challenging the very existence of such a thing. Such narratives exploded the myth of a single, unified black home, even as they set about reimagining and rebuilding it.

Again, personal and collective autobiography are critical here. Raised in a close-knit family with five other siblings (most of whom have worked for Sinbad throughout his career), the comedian once recalled how his mother, a minister's wife, took barefoot children into their home "because she couldn't bear to see [them] going through that kind of life."[1]

Throughout his career, Sinbad has always made a point of delivering wholesome, family-oriented entertainment to his fans. "If my kids can't watch it," he has often said, "I can't do it." When *The Sinbad Show* premiered on Fox, the actor-comic was in the midst of a divorce and custody battle over his two children. He pitched this sitcom about a responsible black father in the hopes of countering representations that "slammed on men."[2]

Sinbad wanted his show to reflect stable homes, he told the press, adding that it was "time people realized that black men *can* be positive role models."[3] Although his sitcom never consisted of the kind of hardcore dramedy seen on shows like *Frank's Place, South Central,* or *Roc,* Sinbad's extratextual remarks revealed that he wished it had. "I don't want to just do comedies," he explained. "I try to deal with issues. Living in America, you can't just do a *Dick Van Dyke Show* or a *Mary Tyler Moore Show.* Kids are dying. There are weapons out there. You *cannot* act like things aren't happening."

On his sitcom, Sinbad played David Bryan, a bachelor and part-time foster home volunteer who decides to adopt twelve-year-old L.J. (Willie Norwood) and his five-year-old sister, Zena (Erin Davis). The key to black people's future, explained Sinbad in an interview with *Jet* magazine, "is not just going to be parenting. It's going to be mentoring, where people who are not even in your family are going to have to go in and help. We're going to accept that responsibility, which we used to do in our culture."[4]

Much of *The Sinbad Show* reflected Bill Cosby's influence. After all the actor's first regular television role had been on the *Cosby* spinoff *A Different World,* and the older comedian remained a mentor for Sinbad long after that show's cancellation. In fact, David Bryan's fictional father, Rudy (Hal Williams), was much like Cliff Huxtable, with his steady and wholesome advice. In addition, a stream of extended-family members, neighbors, and teachers flowed through the Bryan household—just as they had on *Cosby*. Moreover, Sinbad often made improvised references to both Cosby the man and *The Cosby Show*.

Sinbad, like Cosby, also sought to legitimize the notion of non-biological and extended families. Just as Cosby required that his fictional wife speak Spanish (as does his real-life wife, Camille), so too did Sinbad fight for the inclusion of the Latina character Gloria (Salma Hayek) as an apartment manager and occasional babysitter. "I wanted people to see involvement between black and [Latino] people," he explained. "Because we *do* interact. We have *always* interacted. We're at that bottom rung of society together. But you never see us in television unless we're fighting."

At the start of the season, Gloria appeared as a regular cast member. In publicity stills, she held Zena in her arms alongside Bryan family members. Midway through the season, however, her character was abruptly cut from scripts. Sinbad was furious. He was told that she didn't have enough "purpose"—which meant, to his mind, that producers were frustrated by his refusal to sexualize her and make her into David's lover. "I was going to show Gloria and her family," he later explained. "But not in a typical way. She was a college student with goals. They didn't understand how I was trying to define family as being more than a blood relative."

Similar tensions arose as network executives pushed for Sinbad's character to date more often and to "deemphasize the kid thing." In response, Sinbad attempted to shape a semidramatic episode about interracial romance in which his character would date a white woman. "Coat of Many Colors" was written by Sharon Johnson, one of three black writers on an eight-member staff. According to Johnson, executive producer Marc Sotkin gave her free rein to treat the issue seriously. "Don't make it 'We Are The World,'" he told her. She didn't. As a result, the episode was rejected by both the production company, Touchstone, and by Fox.

Such conflicts might have unfolded differently had Sinbad been surrounded by a production team of his own choosing, as was the case, as we shall see, with *Roc*. Due to prior commitments, however, Sinbad was rushed into production on his show and never felt able to hand-pick his staff.[5] Instead, the original teleplay was written and produced by a total of seven white men. Although Sinbad was an executive producer, he lacked real decision-making power.

While Ralph Farquhar (a producer who was brought in at midseason) was African American, it should not be assumed that he spoke for Sinbad. In fact, there were serious philosophical and cultural differences between the two men. In one episode (discussed further below), for example, an elitist black social club was initially going to be an elitist black fraternity. However, since Farquhar had belonged to a black fraternity himself, he was uncomfortable with portraying the discrimination that takes place in such settings. His thoughts about the matter were, however, "totally different from Sinbad's."[6]

After Ralph Farquhar and his partner, Michael Weithorn, left the show, Marc Sotkin was recruited. "I was the fourth executive producer brought onto the show," recalls Sotkin, who is white. "By then, Sinbad was disenchanted with the whole process. I was basically mopping up." During a later phone interview, Sotkin admitted that he had been somewhat bewildered by Disney's (Touchstone's) hiring practices. "When I came on, there were two other white [producers]," he explained, "Arnie Kogen and Tom Weeden. So we were these three middle-aged white guys." After a long pause, he added, "I don't know what the thinking was."

"A season of twenty-two episodes is running eleven to twenty-two million dollars for a company," continued Sotkin, "and I guess they wanted someone who they didn't think was going to crash and burn. . . . But were we the right people to bring in? Probably not. They just didn't have confidence in Sinbad. Let me give you an example," he continued. Sinbad got us [R&B singer] Babyface as a guest. People at Disney didn't even know who he was. . . . I have real regrets about *The Sinbad Show,*" he concluded. "It wasn't friendly and it wasn't pretty."

"This was supposed to be a star-driven show, like *Roseanne,*" explained Sinbad in 1994. "And when you have that kind of show, you're supposed to take somebody's energy and fit the show *around* them. But since there are no black executives and hardly any black writers in the industry, that [rarely] happens with black entertainers . . . because no one understands your lifestyle."

Because of such dynamics, the politics of production on *Sinbad* were intriguing. Like *Cosby, A Different World,* and *The Fresh Prince,* it sought to expose issues of color and caste prejudice among black people—but with far less success. In the remaining pages of this chapter, I want to focus on two such episodes.

The first, called "Shades of Acceptance," opens with Zena, L.J., David, and David's father playing football in the family living room. Entering with bags of groceries, David's mother, Louise Bryan (played by jazz singer Nancy Wilson) expresses disappointment that her granddaughter hasn't been exposed to "little-girl" activities such as ballet and dressing up. Louise suggests that Zena join Dick and Jane, a black social club. For in-group audiences, the name "Dick and Jane" is telling, as it alludes to the real-life Jack and Jill, a prestigious organization mostly composed of upper-income black families.

All of the men in the house object immediately to the idea of Zena's joining Dick and Jane. David, Rudy, and David's best friend, Clarence (T. K. Carter), all agree that the organization is full of "snobby, uptight, bourgie phonies . . . with their noses in the air [who] wear Victorian dresses and . . . walk around asking people to pass the crumpets and tea." But when Zena expresses an interest in "dressing up," David reluctantly agrees to visit Dick and Jane.

At an open house for new members, upper-income attendees discuss the stock market while David wanders uncomfortably through the room. "I haven't seen this many black people wearing sweaters since *Cosby* went off the air," he quips. And when he tries to blend into one group by interjecting a joke, elitist club members respond by launching into conversational French in order to exclude him.

In another circle, a group of women discuss a Sotheby's art auction. "There were some magnificent Monets and Degas," recalls one member. "Actually, I went there to buy a Rubens but I was outbid. . . . Four hundred thousand dollars for a Rubens was a tad out of my range." "Four hundred thousand dollars for a Ruben!" exclaims David. "You need to go down to Willie's Sandwich Shack. You get a reuben *this big* for a buck fifty." As one member of the group turns her head in disgust, David pats the top of her head and her thick, long hair. "Not real," he notes, to her dismay.

Soon David meets Beverly Winters, club president of Dick and Jane. "Oh, you're Louise's son!" she exclaims, glancing at his garish shirt. "I see you take after your father," she suggests disapprovingly. (Apparently David's father was so offensive to club members that his mother was kicked out of the club soon after meeting him.)

The casting of television legend, Diahann Carroll as the snooty Beverly Winters is a fascinating choice here, adding layers of intertextual meaning to the narrative. For viewers familiar with early black shows of the 1960s and 70s, Carroll is best known for her groundbreaking role as the star of *Julia,* a controversial sitcom in which she played a nurse and single mother. For some audiences, the show was discomfiting in that it not only refused the common markers of "blackness" but, even more important, it presented a black woman who was completely content in a white middle-class environment. Not only was Julia portrayed as effortlessly integrated, she seemed not to care about or even to notice her estrangement from a particular black community. In the 1980s, Carroll made an interesting guest appearance on *A Different World* in which her snobbish, upper-class character was referred to as a "product of assimilation."

David bonds with Beverly Winters's husband, Scott (Robert Hooks), in part, because both men agree that Dick and Jane club members are pretentious. "Man, there are some uptight brothers and sisters here," notes David upon meeting Scott. "Yeah, there are, quite a few," responds Winters, a technology trail-blazer and the first to "put Malcolm X on floppy disk," as David notes appreciatively. "Especially that Mrs. Winters," continues David. "She's tighter than a gnat's behind on a lemon wedge." After explaining that Beverly Winters is his wife, Scott reassures David that he too said "pretty much the same thing" upon meeting her.

Soon David and "Scottster" are "ace boon coons," as my mother used to say, golfing together and making plans for joint ventures in computer programming. Everything is going well between the Winters and the Bryans, in fact, until Scott and Beverly's granddaughter, Crystal (Tracy Douglas), comes to visit little Zena. Over play tea, the very light-skinned Crystal announces, "My gran says you're always pretty if you're lighter than a brown paper bag." "What about Johnnie?" asks Zena, gesturing to her brother. "Uh-uh, his skin's too dark." "Hold up!" interjects David, overhearing the conversation. "Wait a minute! Wait a minute! What's goin' on here?" When Crystal responds that she "doesn't know" why she said what she did, David seats himself at the tea table and addresses the girls with typical Cosby finesse:

> DAVID: Let me ask you something: Do you like Barney?
>
> GIRLS: Yes.
>
> DAVID: Why do you like Barney?
>
> CRYSTAL: Because he's friendly and he sings songs . . .
>
> ZENA: And he's purple.
>
> DAVID: He's a dark purple, isn't he? But you still like him, don't you? And if he was light, you'd still like him, too. Right?
>
> GIRLS: Yeah.
>
> DAVID: So you gotta treat people the same as dinosaurs. You got all types of black people. You got yellow. You got brown. You got black. You got albino. All right? Nobody is better than anybody else. We're all black.
>
> L.J.: Yeah . . . [to Crystal] Ya high yella banana!

Unlike *Cosby*'s message of a color-blind society, this scene is deeply rooted within an intraracial context, as is evidenced by L.J.'s in-group reference to light skin. (In the lexicon of African American color descriptors, "high yellow" is right up there with "redbone," both of which have derogatory connotations.) Had David concluded with "We're all American" or "We're all people" rather than "We're all black," the text would have been situated very differently indeed, and the historical weight of these intraracial tensions would have been mitigated by our shared humanity and/or Americanness.[7]

In my interviews with Sinbad, the comedian talked openly about his experiences with color discrimination as a young man. "One of the issues that has always been troubling in my life was [color]. Where my mom's from, in Tennessee, you were fortunate to be light. Where I grew up, though, I was such a militant. I think because of my color, I was *so* militant. By the time I was thirteen, I wanted to be a Black Panther. Brothas would walk up to me—'Yo, yellow nigga'—and I would go off."

In fact, the brown-paper-bag exchange is foreshadowed by an earlier scene further confirming that Beverly Winters is a woman estranged from her "blackness." While shopping for cotillion dresses, David and Zena run into Beverly and Crystal at the mall. The dress Zena has chosen for the party is an African-style gown with a matching head wrap. Beverly Winters disapproves. "That's not the kind of dress one wears to a cotillion," she warns.

Although David Bryan's initial impulse is to sever all ties with Dick and Jane after the brown-paper-bag remark, Rudy Bryan (Hal Williams) convinces his son (à la Cosby) that he can "make a difference" by allowing Zena to wear her African dress. Once again, it is the men—Rudy, David, Scott, and even young L.J.—who uphold cultural authenticity. At the cotillion ceremony, L.J. wears an Islamic skullcap and beats the bottom of a water jug as David emcees Zena's entry. "Yes!" he announces. "Zena Beckley is wearing her garb from Africa. She's gone to the motherland and claimed her blackness. Even though she's yellow, she knows who she is!"

I find it inspiring that this entire speech was completely improvised by Sinbad. Equally fascinating is the fact that this last line is punctuated by a laugh track. Because studio audiences on black shows are generally African American and Latino youths from working-class communities such as Compton (networks are interested, after all, in "authentic" responses), it is unlikely that they would respond in this way.[8]

The moment is reminiscent of a scene on *The Fresh Prince of Bel*

Air in which canned laughter follows Philip Banks's announcement that his son has been accepted into Yale University. Why is this funny? Such awkward moments in black television production serve to illustrate the ways in which white editors, producers, and executives often use humor to mask their ignorance about black experiences and worldviews.

In fact, this entire Dick and Jane script met with resistance at Fox. "Do we really have to deal with this color thing?" Sinbad recalled being asked by executives. "Disney was so scared," he added. "They said, 'Let's just show that *all* Americans have problems.' " But, as Sinbad insisted, the episode was not about *all* Americans. "It was about kids with light skin," he said. "Kids with dark skin."

According to both Sinbad and Ralph Farquhar, some staff writers were not even aware, prior to making the episode, that color prejudice existed among African Americans. In fact, one member of the creative team actually suggested that the show would "work better" if it were about Zena experiencing discrimination as a foster child—something that audiences "could relate to." But intraracial prejudice *is* a central theme in African American experience, and something that black people certainly *do* relate to.

As the words of *Sinbad*'s warm-up comic Lewis Dix demonstrate, colorism among African Americans is deeply ingrained and often unconscious. "I used to be fine," Dix tells the studio audience between takes. "But when you get married you get uglier." The audience laughs. "No, really, I used to be light. But you get darker when you get married. Your nose gets bigger." It is no coincidence that Dix's routine echoes the episode's theme; both narratives are addressing the same in-group audience.

After Zena models her African garb, what follows is a messy chain of events and general goofiness typical of Sinbad's comic style. As David rallies guests to let their weaves down, eat pig's feet, and "be themselves," Beverly Winters flies into a rage. "Stop that jungle music!" she cries.

The final straw is when her daughter announces that she has

fallen in love with the very dark-skinned Clarence. "I have worked too hard," shrieks Beverly Winters, "to let some low-down, no-class, street-hanging, baggy-pants-wearing, nasty, slimy man like you put your hands on her! Never happen! You have no money. You have no education. Don't even *look* at this child!" As mother and daughter exit in a huff, David and Scott Winters agree to continue their business partnership despite the evening's fiasco. "Are we still on for our project?" asks David. "Call me," says Scott under his breath. To which David responds, "I knew you were black."

So while the surface narrative of this episode appears to be a critique of colorism, its ideological premise actually involves a far more complex attack on class mobility and, specifically, black women's response to wealth. Clearly, it is Beverly Winters, and to some extent Louise Bryan, who fail to see the implications of their racial estrangement. The men around them, on the other hand, remain deeply committed to retaining their "Africanity" and working-class authenticity.

(As an aside, this reading of ambitious, deracinated black women is also echoed in an episode of *The Sinbad Show* in which David's ex-girlfriend manipulates and seduces him for financial gain. It is interesting to note that the actress cast in this role, Natalie Venetia Belcon, also played a lying seductress on *The Fresh Prince of Bel Air* during the same season.)

In another episode of *The Sinbad Show,* "Family Reunion," traditional constructions of the black family are again exploded by color and caste differences. The occasion is a Bryan family reunion and barbecue. As relatives gather at David's house, we are again reminded that Louise Bryan comes from a cultured, well-bred family, whereas her husband's working-class relatives are decidedly less refined.

The main source of tension at the affair is Pearl Lee, a light-skinned, tight-lipped relation who complains incessantly and runs disapproving fingers across dusty furniture. When the time comes to take a family photo, Pearl Lee suggests taking the picture without L.J. and Zena "so we can have at least one with just the *real* family." Predictably, Zena and L.J. retreat to their room with hurt feelings; David soon follows.

"Family is more than being a blood relative," he explains to the children, with that now-familiar *Cosby* tone. "It's about making a commitment to support and love people that you care about. I made a commitment to you two. You are my family." What's striking about this episode is not only this explicit attempt to redefine "the black family" but its implicit aesthetic choices as well.

Following the "official" narrative, which ends with a freeze-frame of a Bryan family portrait (including the adopted children), it is as though David Bryan disappears and Sinbad takes over. In fact, the show's final moments read more like a home video than a sitcom. As the family interacts in slow motion to the O'Jays song "Family Reunion," David's fictional family merges (through music and style) with that of a larger African American "imagined community."[9]

Both Sinbad and director Chuck Vinson, who is black, were particularly proud of this montage. As Vinson noted, "It showed the emotion of family unity. Dorothea [Sinbad's real-life sister] started crying when she saw it. We fought like hell with the executive producers to get it on . . . probably because they didn't [even] know the song."

In conclusion, although Sinbad may have intended for his sitcom to follow in the color-blind American family tradition of Bill Cosby, the narratives produced were, like most black productions of the period, richly complicated by nationalist desire. As the text attempted to resurrect the black family, it also asked difficult questions such as: What do we mean by the "black" home anyway? Who gets included? Who gets left out?

The text responded by rewriting "blackness" itself—not necessarily through drama, as might have been the case if Sinbad had had more power—but rather through improvisation, aesthetics, and autobiography. In both the "Shades of Acceptance" and "Family Reunion" episodes, *Sinbad*'s creative team used these elements to create conversations for us alone.[10]

3

Ralph Farquhar's South Central and Pearl's Place to Play: Why They Failed Before Moesha Hit

In this chapter, I use the work of television writer-producer Ralph Farquhar to further illustrate caste and class dynamics in black television. Like *The Fresh Prince* and *Sinbad,* shows produced by Farquhar engaged in head-on ideological battles around economic mobility and color. It should be noted that this chapter is somewhat unique in its discussion of black authorship, given that Farquhar's most controversial show, *South Central,* was actually created by a white man, Michael Weithorn. Although Farquhar shared co-producer and co-creator credits with Weithorn, it was the latter who initially pitched the idea for the show.

"I met with Michael at the suggestion of Rose Catherine Pinkney [a television executive who worked on both *In Living Color* and *New York Undercover*]," recalled Farquhar. "He created the show, so I knew he had the sensibility to do it. Also, he was committed to learning. We did a lot of focus groups with [black] single mothers so we would have accurate and current information. We didn't want the show to look like it came out of a white Hollywood imagination." The dynamics of black authorship become even more intricate when we consider that Weithorn was at that time married to an African American woman.

Having said all this, I refer to *South Central* as a black production for two reasons: one, because it was inextricably wedded to black lives, memories, and experiences; and two, because Farquhar himself was at least half of its creative force. It was his autobiographical history—that is, his memory of color, class, and gender, not Weithorn's—that was clearly engaged in these narratives. I want to make it clear that it is not my intention to dismiss Weithorn's presence in these texts in any way. Rather, I focus on Farquhar because this book is dedicated to exploring the concept of "black" authorship, however mythical that may be.

In fact, Farquhar's insistence (conscious or otherwise) on collective black autobiography was even more dogged than that of Benny Medina, Quincy Jones, or Sinbad. Whereas the latter group of producers sought to reference "blackness" within largely mainstream contexts, Farquhar's texts remained wholly inside their own racial constructs, only rarely allowing entry to crossover audiences.

Before looking at the texts themselves then, I should offer a bit of background on Ralph Farquhar. In the early 1980s the young writer launched his television career as an apprentice on the hit series *Happy Days.* When that stint ended, Farquhar went on to explore the world of feature films, eventually penning the screenplay for *Krush Groove,* a 1985 cult classic. In 1987 Farquhar was hired as a supervising producer on Fox's *Married . . . with Children,* an opportunity that would soon become one of his great career coups.

As Farquhar notes, there was no such thing as an African American executive producer in the 1980s. Although he was only at the start of a long upward climb with *Married,* his supervising producer credit was a fortuitous beginning. We should recall that Fox's offbeat tastes had provided a black writer, Michael Moye, with the opportunity to co-create *Married . . . with Children.* It was only fitting that the network would give Farquhar a chance to produce it.

To his advantage, the series went on to become the longest-running sitcom ever produced. This was important in that its growing success gave Farquhar the leverage he needed to pursue his own agenda. With the *Married* credit under his belt, the producer was able to set about crafting culturally specific shows. In 1988 Farquhar created two pilots for ABC: *Living Large* and *New Attitude.*

Living Large was a dramedy about an aspiring New York artist/hairdresser struggling to make ends meet for his young wife and baby. Produced by Stephen Cannell and Quincy Jones (before Jones had *Fresh Prince* weight to throw around), the show had several serious moments. Needless to say, *Living Large* was rejected by the network for lack of a "companion" show to schedule alongside it.

New Attitude was slightly more successful. In 1990 ABC aired eighteen episodes of this snappy comedy from feature film producers George Jackson and Doug McHenry. Based on the chitlin-circuit stage play *Beauty Shop* the show featured young hairdressers cuttin' up in a black environment. "Maybe we're just three unhip white guys," Farquhar was later told by ABC's heads of programming, "but we don't understand it." The series, they eventually determined, was "too black." "It *was* a raucous black show," agreed Farquhar years later. "And it was one of the earliest shows written and produced by blacks. The network didn't know what to do with it."

Although neither pilot met with long-term success, by 1992, when he left *Married,* Farquhar had achieved a level of respectability all too rare among black producers. That same year he partnered with Michael Weithorn to create his most prized project to date: *South Central.* A dramatic depiction of a working-class mother and her three children, the series was virtually stripped of laugh tracks. Not only did it reject the standard joke-per-page format, the dramedy absolutely refused polite resolutions to issues such as unemployment, poverty, teen sex, homicide, and drug addiction.

Predictably, the show languished on network shelves for years. Although CBS had initially committed to buying it, the "Tiffany network" dropped the ball after viewing the pilot. "You've got to make a decision on whether you're doing a comedy or a drama," said Peter Tortorici, then vice president of entertainment at the network. "We can do an 'important' show or we can do one that gets watched."[1] After calling the series "brilliant," CBS passed, with regrets.

In the meantime, the newly launched *Sinbad Show* was having problems of its own. To help salvage the floundering series, Fox called on now veteran producers, Farquhar and Weithorn, who agreed to come onboard only after signing an historic deal with the network. In exchange for their expertise on *Sinbad,* Farquhar and Weithorn were promised an order for thirteen episodes of *South Central* as a midseason replacement.

This was a crucial moment in the annals of black television. Although unknown to the general viewing public, a unique window of opportunity was being presented to select African Americans during the early 1990s. Because Fox was in desperate need of "urban" viewers to build its name brand, producers such as Farquhar and Weithorn were able not only to create dramatic, collective autobiography, but to actually get such shows on the air. It wasn't that *South Central* was better than *Living Large* or *New Attitude* (although I think it was that, too). What was important here was Fox's short-lived marketing strategy that required African American and Latino audiences.

The premise of *South Central* revolves around Joan Mosley (Tina Lifford), a single mother raising three children in Los Angeles's inner city. Joan's seventeen-year-old son, Andre (Larenz Tate), is a kindhearted teen confronting the terrors and temptations of street life in a way that Will Smith never did. Meanwhile, Tasha (Tasha Scott), age fourteen, faces challenges of her own: acne, boys, identity crises, and the heartbreak of an absent father. Joan's firstborn son, Marcus, was a homicide victim before the season even began. And five-year-old Deion (Keith Mbulo), who refuses to speak, is a troubled foster child—a "crack baby"—adopted by Joan after Marcus's death.

Described by one television critic as "gritty, urban, and down with the streets," *South Central* was deeply unsettling to some viewers. Cinema-verité shots of neighborhood streets were nothing like the bright, staged interiors of typical sitcoms. Disjointed camera angles and ambiguous conclusions were particularly disconcerting for viewers accustomed to cardboard smiles and happy endings. In contrast, the camera offered off-center and unexplained snapshots of black life: a Muslim selling bean pies; "round-the-way" girls skipping rope; a dreadlocked brothah on a park bench; neighbors fanning themselves from a porch.

The series met with immediate controversy following its 1994 debut. While some (mainly African American) viewers lambasted its "negative" representations of drugs and gangs, other (mainly white) fans praised the show's unflinching "realism." Mainstream television critics, generally speaking, raved. Tom Shales of the *Washington Post* called the series the "bravest" since *NYPD Blue,* while the *Los Angeles Times* said it was the very best of Fox's "conveyor belt" of black comedies.[2] From a cultural studies perspective, of course, such mixed reactions held great promise, as they indicated, at the very least, the presence of a richly complicated production.

In the premiere episode of *South Central* we learn that Joan Mosley, a public-school administrator, has been fired due to budget cuts and is entering her fourth week without a paycheck. While shopping for groceries in the black-owned Ujamaa co-op (one of the seven principles of Kwanzaa, meaning "cooperative economics"), Joan is informed that her last check bounced and that she's now on the cash-only list. When Joan protests, Lucille, a sharp-tongued Latina cashier (played by Jennifer Lopez), spits back: "*Mira, no empiezas conmigo, porque no juego!*" ("Look, don't start with me, because *I don't play*!") One is reminded here of Sinbad's critique that Latinos and African Americans are always seen as fighting on television. In this case however the fight is used as a setup to explore, in later episodes, black-Latino solidarity.

We also see how Ujamaa's aesthetics are central to the underlying ideology of the text. On one wall, a Martin Luther King Jr. quote warns: "We shall learn together as brothers or perish together as fools." Another sign promises "Jobs for Guns." For in-group viewers aware of African American history, the co-op is highly reminiscent of 1970s black nationalism. Ujamaa sponsors community services such as free blood-pressure testing and literacy programs, much as the Black Panthers once did. There are other nods to "the movement" and racial solidarity as well: homeless men are hired to work there, and when store manager Bobby Deavers (Clifton Powell) appears, his dashiki and skullcap are in keeping with the store's Afrocentrism.

In mediating the dispute between Joan and Lucille, Deavers soon realizes that Joan is unemployed, and he offers her a job as assistant manager at Ujamaa. Although she is clearly overqualified, Joan eventually accepts the position in order to put food on her family's table. This is a key move, as it grounds the series (and its viewers) in a distinctly black context. Whereas the premiere episode began with Joan begging a white man for a corporate position across town, the Ujamaa job returned her (and us) "home," by providing an opportunity to contribute to the economic and spiritual empowerment of black people.

"Welcome to Ujamaa," says Joan, greeting customers with the store's mantra. "When you support the co-op, you support the community." Before long, Joan has even learned to greet Latino customers in Spanish: "*Cuando sostiene el co-op, sostiene la comunidad.*" Soon she and Lucille have become comrades in the struggle. A good example of this tentative black-Latino alliance is seen in an episode that celebrates "Black Dollar Day" at Ujamaa.

After showing up late for her shift and rolling her eyes repeatedly, Lucille finally tells Bobby Deavers what's on her mind. "I'm sorry. You know, I wasn't sure I should work on Black Dollar Day. I thought it might be Black Cashier Day too. And why is it always 'black' this and 'black' that? What about the brown dollars? . . . Thank you for shopping at Ujamaa," she adds sarcastically, addressing the next customer. "When you support the co-op, you ignore the Latinos in the community."

Such scenes invite Latinos and African Americans to co-create culturally insular dialogues by taking seriously the possibilities of political allegiance, *familia,* and solidarity. "You're right, Lucille," concedes Bobby Deavers. "Latinos should be included too. Next year we'll have a Black Dollar Day and a Brown Dollar Day." Like Sinbad's efforts to incorporate Gloria into the Bryan family, the producers of *South Central* made conscious attempts to redefine what is meant by the "black" community by including Latinos.

I focus next on a two-part episode of *South Central* that, as we shall see below, is thematically linked—although not intentionally—with Farquhar's later creation, *Pearl's Place to Play.* While the surface narrative of this two-part story was both praised and criticized for its daring treatment of gang violence, I propose that most critics and viewers failed to consider the complexities of gender, color, and caste that were also at work in the text.

The first episode begins with Andre riding the bus to Inglewood to see his mentor, Dr. Ray McHenry (Ken Page). Once there, Andre meets Nicole (Maia Campbell), McHenry's young intern. Although they are instantly attracted to each other, there are also caste and class barriers between the teenagers. Nicole is from the wealthy community of Ladera Heights. Andre is from South Central. The only way for him to see her is to ride the bus through gang territory—a practice his mother strictly forbids.

One Sunday, however, Andre convinces Joan to make an exception and allow him to meet Ray, Nicole, and her parents at church. "Come on, Ma," urges Andre. "Gangbangers been drinking forties all night. They too hung over to mess with anybody." But he's wrong. Hours later Nicole's parents are seen waiting impatiently for Andre, who has yet to arrive.

Clearly Nicole's parents are members of the black elite; if they had appeared on *The Sinbad Show,* they would most certainly have belonged to the Dick and Jane club. Nicole's mother is seen wearing a classically tailored pink outfit and matching hat, while her husband is elegantly suited. When Nicole suggests that they go ahead to church while she waits for Andre, her mother looks down her nose as if her daughter had belched aloud: "Young lady, *please.*"

Eventually Andre stumbles in—bruised, bloodied, and without shoes. "I got jacked by a trick-ass punk who stole my gym shoes," he explains to Nicole's dismayed parents, who are as shocked by his language as by the crime. Nicole's mother refuses even to shake Andre's hand, and quickly instructs her husband to gather up their daughter. "I'll see you later, Andre," suggests Nicole hopefully. "Oh, no, you won't," interjects her mother. But Andre doesn't give up so easily. After arranging to meet his "honey dip" again, the seventeen-year-old slinks into his mother's closet and unearths a gun. Then, after concealing the "gat" in the front of his pants, he heads north to Inglewood for the third time.

It is interesting that Nicole's mother is adamantly opposed to Andre, while her father remains relatively silent on the subject. Like Beverly Winter on *The Sinbad Show,* she represents a certain materialism and an estrangement from working-class black people that is constructed as oddly female. To wit, Nicole's mother promises her a Jeep if she stays away from Andre. Nicole agrees. Her father says nothing.

In fact, as Farquhar informed me, his own mother, unlike his father, was also quite "bourgie." "She grew up in Evanston, Chicago," he explained. "There were very few black people there at the time. She went to Evanston Township, which was one of the best high schools in the country, and she spoke real proper. . . . My mother's father played golf, and his wife had very strong Indian features. My father, on the other hand, was as dark as a chunk of coal. My parents had to elope because my mother's parents *hated* the fact that she married my father. My grandmother, who was senile, would talk to the walls at night and say, 'Those Farquhars, those dark people.' That's how she referred to my father."

We see here how color and class overlap into a uniquely African American phenomenon that I refer to here as "caste." "Most shows ignore the dynamics of black families," continued Farquhar. "It's just more acceptable to present us in a white environment, like *Cosby*." But *South Central* was not *Cosby*. Just as Farquhar's parents eloped to escape family disapproval, so too does

Andre creep onto Nicole's roof in order to see her. When he discovers that his buppie girlfriend has been avoiding him for a new Jeep, however, Andre lashes out.

"Rashad is right," he tells Nicole. "You just another bourgie sell-out, thinking you better than everybody else. . . . And you know that [straight] hair ain't nothin' but a ultra perm!" As if the point were not yet clear for viewers, at least four additional scenes refer to Nicole as "bourgie." In one, Nicole asks her best friend, Candy, "Why do you have to act so bourgie?" "Because I am," replies Candy. "And so are you."[3]

A series of events in this two-part episode eventually leads to the end of Andre and Nicole's relationship. In another confrontation on the bus, Andre is shaken by having to show his gun. But he also begins to enjoy the protection it seems to offer, and soon he's in the habit of carrying it—that is, until Bobby Deavers steps in to confront him. "I heard you had an incident on the bus the other day," says Deavers. "Look, I know how it is out there. A little beef escalates into something big, and everybody is carrying guns these days. I wouldn't want [you] to get into that. . . . We gotta keep the black man strong in our community. We're becoming an endangered species."

There is closure to this episode—true to sitcom format. In the end, Andre reassures his mother (who has no idea that he has been "strapped" with her gun) that he's going to do "the right thing." What sets this episode apart from happy-ending sitcoms, however, is actor Larenz Tate's presentational speech, which comes at the show's conclusion. "Guns don't protect you," he warns, facing the camera directly. "They only raise the stakes." As we pull back from this close-up, viewers see that Tate stands in the midst of several dozen equally serious African American faces, also facing the camera. This tag scene further confirms the non-comedic nature of *South Central.*

And yet discussion about the series among viewers, critics, and producers was misleading in that it presented these dramatic episodes as if they were *solely* about guns and gang violence. My point here is that caste differences were also clearly raised. In fact, color and class tensions between Nicole and Andre were more directly autobiographical for Farquhar than were the show's allusions to gangs. Indeed, the series's overt focus on street life, masculinity, and violence was yet another indication of the narrow manner in which "blackness" is marketed, sold, and received.

In the next section of this chapter, we see how Farquhar's subsequent creation, *Pearl's Place to Play,* made color conflicts central to the text's story line. *Pearl's* was a pilot brought into being by four black men: Ralph Farquhar and Calvin Brown Jr. wrote the pilot; rap mogul Russell Simmons was a producer; and Stan Lathan directed. (Michael Weithorn pursued other projects following the cancellation of *South Central.*)

In *Pearl's,* comic Bernie Mac plays Bernie, the owner of a down-home southern diner. His wife Lillian (Angela Means), is an extremely light-skinned woman whose "bourgeois wanna-be" family disapproves of Bernie. Also central to the narrative are Bernie's ex-wife, Jocelyn (Adele Givens), and their daughter, Selina (Countess Vaughn, who later appears on *Moesha*).

What's striking about *Pearl's,* in addition to its color dynamics, is the fact that all of the women and girls surrounding Bernie are schemers, in the habit of manipulating, threatening, coddling and/or seducing Bernie for his money. In the pilot, Bernie is seen serving coffee, grits, and fried chicken to his clientele. Enter Lillian, who's come for his approval to invite her sister and brother-in-law to dinner. But Bernie doesn't care for his color-prejudiced sister-in-law, Vivian (Khandi Alexander). "When we were dating," he reminds his wife, "she told everybody in the neighborhood you had 'jungle fever.'"

An odd bit of business follows. As the couple discusses dinner Lillian offhandedly opens Bernie's cash register. Without a word, Bernie closes the drawer and moves her away—never missing a beat of the conversation. Lillian eventually gets her way by whispering promises of sex in her husband's ear. And later that evening Bernie discovers the real reason for Vivian's visit.

"Vivian," he notes, "you ain't never thought nobody as black as me was cute. Now, what in the hell do you want?"

As it happens, Vivian and her husband want ten thousand dollars for a summer home on Martha's Vineyard (that ever-present symbol of the black elite). "That's the irony," explained Farquhar, who in real life summers at the Vineyard. "They think they're better than he is [because of color] and yet he's got more money!" At the same time that Bernie is being set up by his in-laws, his ex-wife, Jocelyn, is also milking him for cash, demanding alimony payments for first-class trips to Las Vegas.

I want to emphasize that the central ideological tensions of this show lie within the intersections of color, class, and gender. This is again made clear in a street brawl between Marcus (Lillian's proper-speaking, light-skinned son by a previous marriage played by Theodore Borders) and Selina (Bernie's daughter with Jocelyn). "Marcus said my mama is a loud, no-class, low-life," yells Selina. "Selina said my mother was a stuck-up, bourgie wannabe," responds Marcus.

"See, Bernie Mac," explained Farquhar in an interview with me, "is the same complexion as my father. Whereas the woman who played his wife is like your [the author's] complexion—the same as my mother's.[4] Now, black people don't talk about color prejudice a lot, but there are holdover attitudes. We know that."

Some of these holdover attitudes, about skin color, are consciously engaged in Farquhar's work, while others are not. For example, the notion that women require material goods and are willing to lie and scheme to get them is never challenged. The closing tag scene of *Pearl's,* in fact, reproduces such a myth. Bernie owes his daughter $20 but tries to get away with paying her $10. "Uh-uh!" shouts Selina, imitating Rosie Perez in *Do the Right Thing*: "Gimme my money, Mookie!" "All right," agrees Bernie. "You sound just like your mama."

Whereas *South Central* began the fascinating work of exploring intraracial caste differences, *Pearl's Place to Play* went even further by making such dynamics central to the text. In the end, however, both shows were far too in-house for mainstream audiences and timid executives. In fact, *Pearl's* (taped just one month before Fox's cancellations of *South Central, Roc, Sinbad,* and *In Living Color*) was never picked up at all.

"There was a wall between black and white audiences," explained Farquhar. "Black response was very good, but white viewers didn't get it."[5] A critic for *Black Film Review,* however, saw a different reaction at a Los Angeles screening. "Some audience members were upset," he noted. "[Bernie] Mac's ex-wife is a dark-skinned woman who bore him a very dark and boisterous daughter. But his new wife, played by the very funny Angela Means, a tall, light-skinned, long-haired socialite and their very nice, intelligent, fairer-skinned son are just peachey."

On the surface, then, Farquhar's productions appeared to be straightforward critiques of economic mobility among blacks. In actuality, his narratives were knotty struggles with class and racial identity. Indeed, black America's strained relationship with the American dream was made evident in these shows' various references to *Cosby.* "Look, everybody don't live all perfect like you and the damn Huxtables," Andre tells Nicole in *South Central.* "Girl, don't make me take my belt off. I ain't no Bill Cosby," says a character from *Pearl's.*

In 1996 *South Central* had been off the air for over two years. I interviewed Ralph Farquhar in his office at Sunset Studios, where his latest creation, *Moesha,* was being taped for the United Paramount Network (UPN). There was art by Ernie Barnes on the walls, and a desk plaque that read: "Life is more important than show business." Farquhar, who wore a stunningly bright yellow shirt over tailored black slacks, settled into a couch opposite me and proceeded to explain the difference between *South Central* and *Moesha.*

This time Farquhar shared co-creator and co-executive producer credits with two black women: Sara V. Finney and Vida Spears. Of all the shows Farquhar pitched and created, this was his first real commercial success. Charting the evolution of his work, as well as the space it eventually occupied at UPN, reveals much about the politics of black television in the 1990s. For although *Moesha* was highly similar to *South Central* in style and content, there were key differences between the two shows.

"Fox kept calling *South Central* a sitcom," recalled Farquhar. "But it never was. *Moesha* is a sitcom." Put another way, *Moesha* focused on the trials and tribulations of teen life; *South Central* focused on the trials and tribulations of teen life in a low-income, single-parent household in a high-crime black community.

Even when *Moesha* ventured into dramatic story lines involving race, these were produced and marketed in a very different manner than for *South Central*. In one episode, for example, Moesha's friends accuse her of thinking she's "too good for the 'hood" when she dates a white boy. Although the episode was allowed to air (unlike *The Sinbad Show*'s rejected script about interracial dating), its potentially serious premise was buried by UPN's promotional department. "They showed wacky, nonsensical clips," recalled Farquhar, "that were totally unrelated to the story line." What's more, Farquhar was later told that the episode was "over the top" and that UPN was "not interested in issues."

But we should wonder what is lost when television refuses black drama. "*South Central* was the most startling and uncompromising of my shows," noted Farquhar. "*Moesha* is still honest, but it's different tonally . . . in terms of style and production. Like, there's no single-camera stuff in conjunction with the multi-camera, all of which makes [the story] seem more immediate. . . . [And] we button the seams of *Moesha* with jokes, whereas we didn't make that concession on *South Central*."[6] "If you were expecting a laugh a minute," agreed Rose Catherine Pinkney, "that's not what you were going to get. *South Central* had a different cadence and style."

The key difference lies in *South Central*'s autobiographical content and dramatic approach versus *Moesha*'s traditional sitcom format and mainstream story lines. "*Moesha* is different from a woman losing her job and her son going out and getting money from a dope dealer," acknowledged Farquhar. "It's not to say that middle-class kids don't have problems. Just that . . . *South Central* had an air of gloom. With *Moesha,* we've chosen not to go for the grittier side."

Reflecting on his long career in television, Farquhar arrived at this observation: "The biggest fights with networks were not about money or ratings. They were about different ways of seeing the world." In fact, Farquhar's productions occupy an important space at the far end of black television. As bold as Fox claimed to be in the early 1990s, even it was unwilling to stand by such a controversial series as *South Central.* By the time UPN came along, Farquhar had, of course, changed his approach and had consciously crafted a more lighthearted, uncomplicated comedy in *Moesha.*

In 1997, a year after that interview, I found the producer housed at Universal Television with a three-year development deal. Hard at work on several new sitcoms, Farquhar described his latest project as "multicultural" rather than "black." "It takes place in a church which was traditionally white," he explained, "but with integration has become a community of the working class, the underclass, immigrants, Asians, and Latinos." Another concept recently developed by Farquhar was the ABC pilot *Blendin',* about a black upper-class family and the young white female companion they hire to care for their aged patriarch.

Clearly there has been a progression away from strictly black conversations and settings for Farquhar—which raises interesting questions. Is this trend the result of purely market-driven considerations, the changing positionality of Farquhar himself, or the shifting autobiographies of viewers? Insofar as real-life African Americans confront increasingly integrated settings, our texts begin to wrestle with these memories as well as racially insular ones. As we move toward the end of the 90s, the question "What is black?" becomes even more enigmatic. Our stories, it seems, must work harder to keep up.

Part 2

Gender and Sexuality

"Yo-Yo is flanked by members of her crew, the Intelligent Black Women's Coalition, in black T-shirts emblazoned with Yo-Yo's woodcut visage as Lady Liberty. The girls stand rigid like Fruit of Islam sentinels, faces severe, shoulders squared. 'Brothers in the house, you hear what I'm saying?'

. . . But in a far corner, on the second level, a teen in Kente and a small brass ankh trades a glance with an equally lit homey and shouts. 'Yo, bitch,' he yells, breaking off into cascading laughter, 'get off the stage!'"

From "This One's for the Ladies"
in No Crystal Stair *by Lynell George*

4

Sheneneh, Gender-Fuck, and Romance: Martin's Thin Line Between Love and Hate

In the following two chapters, I discuss *Martin* and *Living Single* in an interrelated manner, paying close attention to the extratextual contexts of actors Martin Lawrence (*Martin*) and Queen Latifah (*Living Single*). My argument is that the real-life politics and documentary experiences of these celebrities, as well as their respective stand-up comedy, feature film, and musical performances, contributed rich and unexpected layers of meaning to the shows in which they starred. Moreover, I propose that the autobiographical dynamics of gender and sexuality in both Lawrence and Latifah's lives played significant roles (conscious or otherwise) in shaping reception practices among in-group viewers. By reception practices I mean the ways in which audiences make meaning of, respond to, and interact with various texts. For example, an analysis of reception practices surrounding these shows might look at the real-life adaptation of various phrases used by Martin Lawrence in everyday conversations ("You go, girl!" for example), or the fact that the majority of viewers watching *Living Single* were women.

While Martin Lawrence developed a real-life reputation for

misogyny and abuse of women, both on and off the set of his show, Latifah was known as the antidote to hip-hop sexism. A widely respected rapper, she carried with her a long history of resistance to macho bravado and, despite her protests to the contrary, was labeled both a feminist and a lesbian. It is ironic that the controversial sexual politics in both Lawrence and Latifah's lives have been so widely publicized, particularly since both *Martin* and *Living Single* set out to address precisely these themes. In marketing and publicity campaigns for both sitcoms, *Martin* was touted as "the black male perspective" on relationships, while the "female response" was its companion show, *Living Single.*

My argument regarding *Martin* is threefold. First, I suggest that the show reveals a deep-seated obsession with what Lawrence refers to as "love-hate" relationships. Second, I propose that the antiwoman hostility expressed on the series is masked by the show's "romantic" pretext as well as by Lawrence's use of drag, or gender-fuck.[1] And third, I explore the idea that *Martin* (as well as a number of other Lawrence productions) both engages and reproduces the comic's real-life controversies with women—creating critical sites upon which to explore race, sexual violence, autobiography, and representation.

The premise of *Martin* revolves around Philadelphia radio deejay Martin Payne and his girlfriend, Gina Waters (Tisha Campbell). *Martin* defenders often argued that the show was the first to feature a young, professional black couple in love, and were understandably pleased to see such a rare representation on prime-time television. The character of Martin certainly was romantic, clearly and unabashedly devoted to his "boo," Gina. And yet I propose that it was precisely this romantic vision of love which served to conceal and even mitigate the show's larger misogyny.

If we take a random sampling of the show's episodes from the 1993–94 season, an interesting pattern emerges. Many storylines suggested that women are sexual objects to be displayed and ogled. Others presume that there is a "natural" and instinctive need for men (and occasionally women) to possess and control their lovers. Some examples: (1) Martin arranges for Gina, a symbol of his success, to have a beauty makeover before his high school reunion. "You are my trophy girl," he coos; (2) Gina accepts emotional abuse and hard labor in order to avoid Martin's wrath; (3) Martin berates Gina for her failure to cook Thanksgiving dinner; (4) Martin decides to get in better physical shape and forces Gina to do the same; (5) Martin is jealous of Gina's friendship with a man named Wallace and assumes she's having an affair; (6) Martin challenges real-life boxer Tommy Hearns to ten rounds after he makes a pass at Gina; (7) Martin accuses Gina of having sex with another man and, after "hunting her down" at a business conference, vows to kill her.

Like Lucy Ricardo in *I Love Lucy,* Gina's physical comedy is often predicated on a certain fear of punishment. In such episodes, Gina's best friend, Pamela James (Tichina Arnold), functions much as Ethel Mertz does, by warning: "Martin gon' kill you." In order to coax her man back to a less threatening self, Gina often resorts to trickery, home cooking, and especially sex. It is helpful to compare Gina's characterization with that of Pam, who is portrayed as a "man-hater," particularly during the show's early seasons. Martin berates Pam at every opportunity, often referring to her as unfeminine, hairy, and animal-like. A typical crack is this:

> PAM: Why can't I find at least a half-decent man?
> [Pause]
> MARTIN: Don't you have mirrors at home?

But Pam certainly *is* attractive to men. She and Gina simply respond to relationships differently. In episode number five described above, for example, it was actually Pam to whom the other man was attracted, not Gina. But while Gina is busy placating a jealous Martin with special high-heeled pumps and open legs, Pam's response to the same stilettos is to look directly at the camera with disgust. Pam and Gina also differ in their professional lives. Although both are career-oriented, Pam is less willing to compromise her autonomy for a relationship. Martin, believing that Gina's independence is a result of Pam's influence, clearly resents her for it.

In short, Martin's interactions with Pam represent a key site of ideological struggle. In one unusual 1994 episode featuring a dream sequence, Pam shows up at Martin's apartment wearing seductive lingerie. Despite himself, Martin is turned on by his nemesis. "It's a thin line between love and hate," he tells her, foreshadowing his 1996 self-penned and -directed feature film whose title is taken from the 1971 classic soul ballad by the Persuaders. With that, Pam draws an imaginary line in the carpet with her foot as her negligee falls open. Finally, Martin succumbs to his desire and surprises even himself by taking her into his arms.

And then he wakes up screaming.

On the subject of his nightmare, even Martin's monosyllabic neighbor, Bro'man, waxes philosophical: "You know, Fraud [Sigmund Freud] 'n' 'em . . . the white philosph' . . . used to say that dreams are like repressed desires. Or the things we wish we could have." Terrified by Bro'man's theory that he might subconsciously lust for Pam, Martin decides that the only solution is to return to bed and face his fears.

Back in his dream once again, Martin lays Pam's body, trembling with desire, across his bed. Moving toward the door, he then locates a dangling rope and pulls. Suddenly a two-ton weight crashes down from the ceiling, killing Pam instantly. Thus relieved of his unthinkable yearnings, Martin's nightmare is over and he can return to a sound sleep.[2]

As Gina strives for personal and professional autonomy, she too is subjected to Martin's wrath. This tension is often played out in episodes that pit Gina the "career woman" against Martin's mother, who is played by Lawrence in drag. A "legitimate" matriarch, Mrs. Payne is known for tending to her son's every need. When Pam and Gina argue that women should not be expected to cook on Thanksgiving, for example, Martin recalls his mama's black-eyed peas and, narrowing his eyes at Pam, spits: "You women of the nineties have just gotten *lazy.*"

In another episode Mrs. Payne descends on her son's household to nurse him through his cold, because Gina is too busy to do so. "The problem with women today," booms Mama Payne, is that they're no longer willing to work seven jobs like she once did. Gina protests that she's not a "superwoman." To which, Martin responds by vomiting at her feet.[3]

In addition to Gina, Pam, and Mrs. Payne, there is another female character who warrants consideration: Martin's neighbor, Sheneneh Jenkins, also played by Lawrence in drag. Initially developed for Lawrence's stand-up comedy act, Sheneneh is a stereotypical caricature of a ghetto "homegirl." With her grossly exaggerated buttocks and colored hair extensions, some have compared her to Flip Wilson's character Geraldine.[4] But as Lawrence told one reporter, Sheneneh represents the "round-the-way girls" he grew up with. "That's my niece and sisters," he explained. "A lot of people don't understand the way they act or why they wear the big, big earrings and things like that. . . . I had never seen a show that gave that type of woman a voice."[5]

Like Pam, Sheneneh (who owns a beauty salon) also prides herself on her emotional and financial autonomy. Like Pam, she too is portrayed as sex-starved. Although Sheneneh has a boyfriend ("LaFonne from the ghetto" as the script reads) she is often seen lusting after other men, such as Todd Bridges, the former child actor from *Diff'rent Strokes,* the rapper Kid from Kid N' Play, or even Martin.

Representations of Sheneneh, Mrs. Payne, Gina, and Pam perform interwoven functions within the text. Their interactions represent dynamic struggles over how "we" define black womanhood. Mrs. Payne, famous for "going off" in defense of her son, is arguably the most grotesque. Upon hearing of injustices (real or imagined) against her son, she has been known to fall out or faint with arms and legs spread-eagled and girdle exposed, to break into spontaneous somersaults, and even to eat furniture. As we have seen, Pam is generally regarded as beastlike by Martin, and Sheneneh is hopelessly mannish despite her devoted attention to hair and nails. To wit:

> GINA: Sheneneh, why do you have to start a fight with everybody who walks down this hall?
>
> PAM: Yes. Why don't you try to act like a *lady* sometimes?
>
> SHENENEH: Whoa, whoa! [pointing a garish red fingernail] Let me try to tell you something, all right? I don't need to act like no lady, all right? I am a lady. And I'll prove it. I'll bust you in your head right now.

One of the key contradictions of gender representation in *Martin* is that while Pam, Sheneneh, and Mama Payne are constructed as strong, independent, "authentic" black women, they are also represented as inherently unwomanly. In a particularly telling episode, Gina and Pam, both senior executives at the same marketing company, apply for membership in the Ladies League of Detroit. "It's a woman's club?" asks Martin, leading up to the obligatory insult: "How you gonna get in, Pam?"

But the battle for black female representation is not waged by Martin in this episode. Rather, Sheneneh and her friend Loquita are recruited for that purpose. And ironically, they *do* manage to become clubwomen—not because of their "femininity" but because, unlike Gina and Pam, they are able to help the "ladies" of the League recapture their emotional and sexual autonomy.

As stated in the beginning of this chapter, the documentary persona of Martin Lawrence is central to my readings of his show. For this reason, I want to turn now to his highly publicized conflicts with *Martin* co-star, Tisha Campbell.

On November 22, 1996, during taping for *Martin*'s fifth season, Campbell surprised cast and crew members by walking off the set and vowing never to return. Two months later Campbell filed a lawsuit against Lawrence in which she charged the comic with "repeated and escalating sexual harassment, sexual battery, verbal abuse, and related threats to her physical safety." Campbell also charged HBO executives Christopher Albrecht and Russell S. Schwartz with "negligent and intentional infliction of emotional distress."

Problems began, according to legal documents filed by Campbell's attorneys, during the show's first season, when the actress rejected Lawrence's romantic advances. During the second season, Lawrence "became increasingly manic and volatile" and would "often and easily, fly into uncontrollable fits of rage for no apparent or rational reason." The abuse intensified during the third season, said the documents, as Lawrence "humiliated and abused Campbell in front of the entire cast and crew on so many occasions that . . . she needed to be hospitalized due to the stress he caused her."

During the fourth season, Lawrence's "mood swings" were so severe that the cast and crew were "terrified" to work with him. It was during this season that Campbell requested a lock on her dressing room door—a request that HBO ignored. Campbell claimed that by the fifth season, Lawrence was "simply out of control" and would often "grope her, force his tongue into her mouth, and simulate sexual intercourse between takes." Although Campbell now asked that an emergency "panic" button be installed in her dressing room, HBO again ignored her requests.

Campbell's court documents further describe Lawrence's conduct as an "apparent obsession," claiming that he "focused lust, anger and violent tendencies" on her to the point that she "felt she had no choice" but to leave—especially after Lawrence's "most hysterical outburst to date," on November 22, 1996. Indeed Campbell's description of that day's events was corroborated by others on the set, who reported that Lawrence arrived at work extremely agitated. After physically confronting one cast member, he turned his attention to Campbell and approached her "with such rage that she was terrified and concerned for her safety."

According to sources who spoke to me on condition of anonymity, Lawrence has suffered for a number of years from a medical condition known as bipolar disorder (another name for manic-depression), which results in wild mood swings. This condition is reportedly exacerbated both by Lawrence's refusal to take prescribed psychotropic medication and by his use of recreational drugs.

My goal in discussing such autobiographical details is to reveal some of the ways in which hostility toward women is manifested in Lawrence's cultural productions, whether as reflections of Lawrence's basic attitude towards women, as a result of his diagnosable mental disorder, his drug use, or a combination of all three. I also want to highlight the processes, conscious and otherwise, by which African American viewers interacted with such narratives.

I begin with Lawrence's failed engagement to actor Lark Voorhies (*How to Be a Player*) in the early 1990s. During the course of my research, I was told by a reputable producer that Lawrence was known to have hit Voorhies during their relationship. After the breakup, Lawrence told members of the press that he was "depressed" and his spirits were low. Eventually he called on a woman "from his past," Patricia Southall, who married Lawrence and gave birth to their daughter, Jasmine Page.

In May of 1996 Lawrence was apprehended after an unusual public outburst in which he stood in a busy Los Angeles intersection shouting at passersby and carrying a loaded gun. Witnesses say that the comic had stopped at a nearby car wash and had been "cracking jokes . . . like he didn't know which way was up." As one onlooker observed, Lawrence's appearance that morning was like that of a "madman." The comic was hospitalized at Cedars-Sinai Medical Center, where his personal physician, Dr. William Young, initially attributed his behavior to a "seizure" but later changed the diagnosis to "dehydration and exhaustion."

Two months later Lawrence was again detained, this time for attempting to board a Phoenix-bound plane with a loaded 9mm Baretta. According to Southall, her husband later checked into Sierra Tucson, an Arizona drug rehabilitation center, but left after only two days. In September of 1996 Southall packed up her nine-month-old daughter and "went into hiding." According to legal documents filed by Southall, Lawrence was combining prescription medication with "almost daily" marijuana use.

On the morning of November 21, 1996, the comic "barged into his estranged wife's hotel room," according to Southall's statement, threatening "to kill her and her entire family while displaying a firearm." In fact, the comic "became so enraged and out of control that he kicked and broke a marble tile wall."

It probably came as no surprise to Campbell, who had received word of the incident, when Lawrence appeared on the set of *Martin* in a "turbulent emotional state" the following morning. Although the actress pleaded with HBO executive Chris Albrecht to postpone taping, she was refused. In the end, it was Lawrence's violence toward Southall and his unpredictable state that morning, coupled with Lawrence's ongoing abuse of Campbell, that prompted her walkout.

Southall eventually obtained a restraining order against her husband, and the couple is now divorced. In March 1997 Tisha Campbell surprised viewers by returning to *Martin* to tape the remaining episodes of the show's final season. Attorneys for both sides refused to comment on the case, and an HBO press release said only that: "All parties have resolved their differences. All other details are confidential."

While some have challenged Campbell's claims against Lawrence, I have found far more sources—cast, crew and professional colleagues—willing to support her version of events than Lawrence's.[6] It is here that reception practices become especially intriguing. While producers, directors, and actors working within the film and television industries invariably expressed faith in Campbell's claims, the tendency among viewers (as reflected in the black press and in anecdotal conversations) was to support Lawrence. In a particularly shocking radio talk show on Los Angeles' KJLH, for example, callers bashed Campbell repeatedly, accusing her of both man-hating and gold-digging. Not surprisingly, neither the host nor his listeners appeared to have reviewed any of the court documents filed by Southall or Campbell.

In the final pages of this chapter, I turn to several of Lawrence's other productions. While the actor has appeared in many feature films (such as *Do the Right Thing, House Party, Boomerang, Bad Boys,* and *Nothing to Lose*), I shall focus only on those in which he exercised significant authorship and creative control, such as *One Night Stand,* a 1989 HBO special; Russell Simmons's *Def Comedy Jam* on HBO, which the comic hosted from 1992 to 1993; *You So Crazy,* a 1994 concert film; a 1994 monologue on NBC's *Saturday Night Live;* and Lawrence's feature film debut, *A Thin Line Between Love and Hate.*

It is absolutely stunning to me that all of these texts share a common presentational persona: that of a young man who finds himself repeatedly trapped in "love-hate" relationships. In both *One Night Stand* and *You So Crazy,* Lawrence describes himself as a guy who loves relationships but "can never get the shit right." Both monologues depict "crazy, deranged" brothas: jealous, possessive types who stalk their lovers and wives, threatening to beat or kill them should they try to leave. "I should crack your muthafucking forehead," says one Lawrence character after a breakup. "I told her ass," says another when his girlfriend goes to a club without him. "I'll kill everybody up in this muthafucker!"

Oddly, Lawrence slips in and out of the first and third person in describing these "deranged" brothahs, only later admitting that he's speaking of himself. "I was very good on first impressions," he explains in *You So Crazy.* "Like the first couple of months, I was the nicest muthafucker. Before all that insecurity, deranged, crazy shit sunk in." Such an admission, coupled with Lawrence's alleged real-life interactions with women, makes for provocative studies in intertextuality.

Lawrence's 1994 guest host appearance on *Saturday Night Live* inspired further controversy for its crude monologue about female body odor and precoital hygiene. Although most West Coast viewers never saw the show (it was not broadcast there after NBC received almost two hundred complaints from East Coast viewers, who because of time zone differences see it three hours earlier), the material was on a par with comments presented that same year in *You So Crazy.*

In Lawrence's concert film, he chastizes women for failing to clean themselves after a bowel movement, and for having the nerve to come to bed with their "pussy smelling like bacon bits." Such hostility echoes that of Martin Payne toward Pam, whom he often accuses of attracting roaches, having bad breath, and not tending to her nappy hair (the "beady-bees").[7]

In *A Thin Line Between Love and Hate,* Lynn Whitfield co-stars as Brandi, a successful realtor obsessed with nightclub promoter Darnell (Lawrence). According to Lawrence, this was to be a story that turned the tables on abusive, womanizing men. The film, he said, was "about a smart, beautiful . . . and functioning psychotic who forces her boyfriend to see that there are dire consequences to hurting someone."[8] Ironically Doug McHenry, one of the film's producers, called *Thin Line* "the male side to the 'Waiting to Exhale' coin—as if our only options were hysteria, desperation, neediness and/or abuse."[9] Although *Thin Line* was billed as a "black *Fatal Attraction,*" there was one key difference: this was a *comedy,* despite the fact that Whitfield's character (a survivor of domestic abuse) was not exactly comic material. "A man . . . plays with us until he thinks we're no fun anymore," she tells Darnell, pointing a gun to his head. "I'm gonna shoot you for all women." "That bitch is crazy," cackled the brothah seated behind me in the theater.[10]

After Tisha Campbell's departure from *Martin,* Lawrence invited Lynn Whitfield to reprise her role as the "crazy, deranged" lover of *A Thin Line* on his sitcom. Whitfield acquiesced, providing an encore performance of a woman obsessed, who is again carted off (smeared lipstick and all) to a mental institution. It is indeed striking that this theme of obsessive, love-hate relationships—addressed in Lawrence's feature film, concert films, and television productions—is all but ignored in popular conversations about *Martin,* which is generally credited with portraying "positive" male-female interactions.

It is also important to note that Lawrence's documentary, presentational, and fictional personas are clearly positioned within a young, male-oriented, hip-hop context. Not only did he serve as host of Russell Simmons's raunchy *Def Comedy Jam* from 1992 to 1993, but in his sitcom as well, there were countless celebratory references to "gangsta" rap, the films of Spike Lee, and "heroic" male figures such as Mike Tyson.[11] I believe that our collective interpretations of such texts have powerful implications for African American audiences. As we struggle with questions of authorship and autobiography, it becomes important to ask: What "black" experience does Lawrence speak to? And why do so many African American viewers seem to identify with and derive pleasure from such narratives?

Far from some idealized notion of a "positive" relationship, gender dynamics between Martin and Gina were really about power and patriarchal desire. One would think—based on viewing patterns among black audiences, who ranked *Martin* number four in 1993 according to Nielsen—that the show was merely a fun-loving depiction of a young, professional couple in love. The stakes here are about more than entertainment. They're about who we allow to dance inside our imaginations and why. They're also about struggling with, and challenging, the ways in which Martin Lawrence's memories and fantasies are our own as well.

5

Living Single and the "Fight for Mr. Right": Latifah Don't Play

There is an episode of *Martin* in which Lawrence's character is prompted by his "boys" to prove a point. While working out at the gym, Martin removes his wedding ring to show his best friends, Tommy and Cole, that he can still get "da honeys." Sure enough, writhing girl-toys flock to his side mere seconds after the gold band disappears. This scene illustrates why it was appropriate that *Martin* served as the lead-in for *Living Single:* Both shared the premise that the world is teeming with black women who'll do just about anything to land a single, and preferably rich, man.[1]

In this chapter I want to highlight three contradictory ideological forces at work in *Living Single.* The first is what I call the "desperation theme," which is based on the market-driven theory that black audiences appreciate regressive representations of women and which was touted by network executives riding the wave of Terry McMillan's best-selling 1992 novel *Waiting to Exhale.* The second is a moderate feminism inspired by the autobiographical vision of *Living Single*'s creator, Yvette Lee Bowser. And the third is a radical womanism presented, more unconsciously than not, through the fictional, presentational, and documentary personas of Queen Latifah.

In an interview with *Ebony* magazine, Bowser said that she wanted to write and produce a show about her own life experiences, her girlfriends, and "the ups and downs of being twenty-something."[2] Because Bowser is a sucessful, independent woman, relatively sympathetic to feminist aims, her characters reflected this sensibility.

According to Bowser, these *Living Single* characters were extensions of different parts of herself: Regine (Kim Fields) is a materialistic fashion horse; Khadijah James (Queen Latifah) is a self-made entrepreneur who publishes her own magazine, *Flavor;* Synclaire James (Kim Coles) is Khadijah's dimwitted but adorable cousin; and Maxine Shaw (Erika Alexander), the ever-present neighbor, is a ruthless attorney who thrives on large quantities of food and sex. In addition, Kyle Barker (T. C. Carson), another neighbor, is a direct play on Kyle Bowser, then director of creative affairs at HBO Independent Productions and the man who would become Bowser's husband.

In television, of course, there is no such thing as absolute creative power—black, female, or otherwise. So Bowser's *conscious* intention to represent black female desire did not always succeed. In this case, there were other forces involved in the production and reception of *Living Single* that interacted with and, at times, overshadowed her autobiographical vision. One was the popular narrative of the desperate black woman; another was the radical womanism inspired by Queen Latifah.[3]

I begin with a brief history of the show. A comedy about four girlfriends sharing a New York brownstone, *Living Single* was born, like most network series, of pragmatic concerns: The production company, Warner Brothers, had what is known as a "holding deal" with both Kim Fields and Queen Latifah, and it needed to find a television pilot to showcase their talents. Because Fields and Latifah urged the studio to meet with at least one black woman writer (a not unreasonable request given that the show to be created was about black women), television history was made: Yvette Lee Bowser (who had worked previously on *A Different World* and *Hangin' with Mr. Cooper*) became the first African American woman to create a successful prime-time series for network television.

We might speak then of black female authorship as something of an executive "accident" in the case of *Living Single.* While neither Warner Brothers nor Fox intentionally set out to create a feminist-minded narrative, the mere act of hiring an African American woman effectively created a space within which collective black female autobiography could potentially thrive.[4] *Living Single,* in other words, presented an unprecedented opportunity to experiment with black female subjectivity on a weekly basis.

At the same time, however, the tension between Bowser's autobiographical impulse and market-driven sensibilities was evident from the start. For example, a revealing bit of *Living Single* trivia involves the battle over the show's title. Initially dubbed *My Girls* by Bowser, the name was changed to *Living Single* by network executives in order to avoid what they feared would amount to male alienation. With the change came a whole host of narrative shifts. Contrary to Bowser's intentions, the show went from being a slice-of-life comedy about girlfriends to a narrative about the "male quest," or the "Fight for Mr. Right" as one two-part episode was dubbed. From its inception, *Living Single* charged head-on, at Fox's urging, toward the imagined *Waiting to Exhale* audience.

Indeed, Bowser admits that the initial impulse behind *Living Single* was in response to Fox's request for something "along the lines" of McMillan's novel. And *Waiting to Exhale* is essentially—as the jacket cover reminds us—a story about "four black women waiting for the men who will finally make things right." As Bowser told *Ebony:* "*Exhale* was definitely an inspiration for the networks to realize that there was a voice out there that people wanted to hear, a black female voice in particular. The popularity of the book helped pave the way for this show."[5] Almost immediately, *Living Single* skyrocketed to the number one spot among African American viewers.

As the following sampling of story lines reveals, a number of episodes from the show's first year portrayed the women as hopelessly obsessed with men: (1) Regine's new man, Brad, is married; (2) Regine's new man, Patrick, has a daughter; (3) Max dates the man Regine has just broken up with; (4) Max, who is twenty-six, is embarrassed to admit that she has been seeing a handsome eighteen-year-old student; (5) a photographer who works with Khadijah is depressed because she broke up with her boyfriend and hasn't done "the wild thing" in a long time. Basically Fox executives chose to focus on male-oriented episodes the first season, as Bowser told me, because they felt these were "stronger."

In this chapter, I propose that the radical womanist persona of Latifah provided an implicit challenge to both *Martin*'s mythical black macho and the regressive politics of female desperation evident in so many episodes of *Living Single.* It was no coincidence, for example, that the only three episodes of the show's first season that did *not* center around men featured Latifah's character, Khadijah James, as an independent entrepreneur: (1) Khadijah asks her lawyer friend, Maxine, to represent her in court; (2) Maxine loans Khadijah money; (3) Synclaire, Khadijah's cousin and employee, feels unappreciated at work and quits.

In order to explore this implicit womanism evoked by Latifah's persona, I borrow from film theorist Christina Lane's 1995 essay "The Liminal Iconography of Jodie Foster," which was published in *The Journal of Popular Film and Television.* In her essay, Lane argues that there is "a strategic sexual liminality" surrounding Jodie Foster. Inherent in this liminality, says Lane, is a refusal to submit to polarized notions of gay-straight or masculine-feminine, a refusal that also works to destabilize fixed gender identities in Foster's films.[6] I find Lane's thesis enormously useful in that it allows us to "read" Foster in a dynamic, intertextual manner—as do viewers.

Debbie Allen, writer-director-producer extraordinaire and the impetus behind *A Different World*'s look at such serious issues as intraracial color discrimination, date rape, and South African apartheid. COURTESY OF DEBBIE ALLEN.

The Fresh Prince of Bel Air cast in its second incarnation. Clockwise from top left: James Avery as Philip Banks; Daphne Maxwell Reid as Vivian Banks (replacing Janet Hubert-Whitten); Joseph Marcell as Geoffrey, the butler; Alfonso Ribeiro as Carlton Banks; Will Smith as himself; Tatyana M. Ali as Ashley Banks; and Karyn Parsons as Hilary Banks. PHOTO COURTESY OF NATIONAL BROADCASTING COMPANY, INC.

Legendary music and television producer Quincy Jones, who was responsible, with partner David Saltzman, for hits such as *The Fresh Prince of Bel Air*, *In the House*, and *Vibe*. COURTESY OF GREG GORMAN AND QUINCY JONES.

Cast of *In Living Color,* the show that set the stage for Fox's successful run of black programming: Keenen Ivory Wayans (top right) in his wildly irreverent role as creator, executive producer, director, and star; clockwise from Wayans are Jim Carrey, who went on to box office fame; Kim Wayans, currently starring in NBC's *In the House;* T'Keyah Crystal Keymah; David Alan Grier; Kelly Coffield; Damon Wayans; and Tommy Davidson. COURTESY OF KEENEN IVORY WAYANS AND FOX BROADCASTING.

Cast of the short-lived *Sinbad Show,* which aired during Fox's 1993-94 season. Clockwise from top: T.K. Carter as Clarence; Salma Hayek as Gloria; Erin Davis as Zena; Sinbad as David Bryan; and Willie Norwood as Little John.
COURTESY OF SINBAD ADKINS AND FOX BROADCASTING.

Producer Ralph Farquhar who created, together with partner Michael Weithorn, the 1994 dramedy *South Central.* Farquhar later went on to create *Moesha,* starring pop sensation Brandy. The sitcom was his first commercial success, and the flagship for the United Paramount Network's (UPN) early programming. COURTESTY OF RALPH FARQUHAR.

The besieged family of *South Central.* From left: Tasha Scott as Tasha; Keith Mbulo as the silent Deion; Tina Lifford as "Mama" Joan Mosley; and Larenz Tate as Andre Mosley. COURTESY OF RALPH FARQUHAR AND FOX BROADCASTING.

Cast of *Martin*. From left to right: Thomas Mikal Ford as Tommy; Tisha Campbell as Gina; Martin Lawrence as Martin; Carl Anthony Payne II as Cole; and Tichina Arnold as Pam. COURTESY OF HBO/HIP AND FOX BROADCASTING.

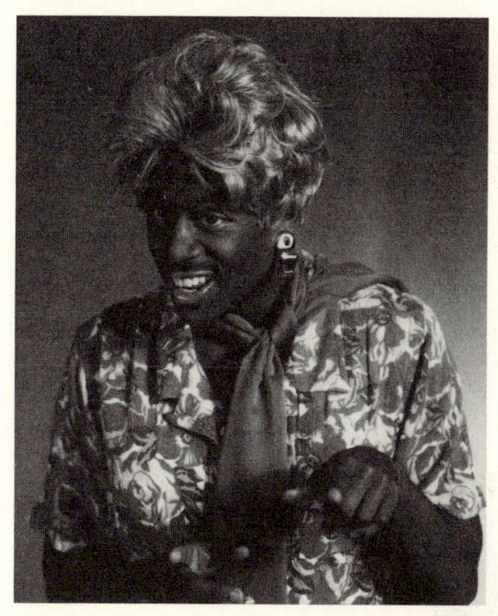

Martin Lawrence as two of his many alter-ego characters: Mama Payne (above) and "round-the-way girl" Sheneneh. COURTESY OF HBO/HIP AND FOX BROADCASTING.

Yvette Lee Bowser, creator of *Living Single,* and the first African American woman to launch a successful prime-time series for network television. The producer is shown here with husband, Kyle Bowser, who, as former director of programming for HBO/HIP, was the executive in charge of both *Martin* and *Roc.* COURTESY OF KYLE AND YVETTE LEE BOWSER.

The first to win *Living Single*'s "Fight for Mr. Right" was Synclaire (Kim Coles). Also pictured (clockwise from center) are John Henton as Overton, the groom; Gladys Knight and Antonio Fargas as his parents; Queen Latifah as Khadijah James; T. C. Carson as Kyle Barker; Erika Alexander as Maxine Shaw; Kim Fields Freeman as Regine Hunter; and Ron O'Neal and Denise Nicholas as parents of the bride.

TOP Cast of *Roc.* From left to right: Charles S. Dutton as Roc Emerson; Rocky Carroll as Joey Emerson; Alexis Fields as Sheila Hendricks; Carl Gordon as Andrew Emerson; and Ella Joyce as Eleanor Emerson. COURTESY OF HBO/HIP AND FOX BROADCASTING.

BOTTOM Rap star Tone Loc in a guest appearance as Ronnie, the neighbor who tries to help Roc remove a crack house from the community. COURTESY OF HBO/HIP AND FOX BROADCASTING.

The ever-evolving cast of *New York Undercover* in its second season. Clockwise from left: Patti D'Arbanville-Quinn as Lieutenant Virginia Cooper; Lauren Velez as Detective Nina Moreno; Michael DeLorenzo as Detective Eduardo Torres, and Malik Yoba as Detective J. C. Williams.

A scene from Damon Wayans's drama *413 Hope Street,* in which Antonio (Jesse L. Martin) confesses to his wife, Angelica (Dawn Stern), that he may have contracted the AIDS virus. COURTESY OF DAMON WAYANS AND FOX BROADCASTING.

Bentley Kyle Evans, a former writer/producer on *Martin* in his office on the Warner Bros. lot. Evans, who began his television writing career on *Martin*, went on to become creator and executive producer of WB's *The Jamie Foxx Show*. COURTESY OF BENTLEY KYLE EVANS AND TRISH MARTIN.

The creative team for *The Jamie Foxx Show* is a far cry from all white writing staffs of the 1980s and early 1990s. Clockwise beginning with man in foreground: Cooper James, Kenny Smith, Kevin Boyd, Craig Davis, Bentley Kyle Evans, Bennie Richburg, Jr., Sandy Frank, Kyra Keene, Arthur Harris, Edward Evans. (Not pictured is Janine Sherman). COURTESY OF BENTLEY KYLE EVANS AND TRISH MARTIN.

Like Foster, Latifah has also been associated with nontraditional representations of femininity, sexuality, and power. Because of her own brand of "sexual liminality," she too has entered (whether willingly or not) into a discourse around both feminism and lesbianism. And like Foster, both Latifah's public and private personas reveal an "ability to slide up and down the registers of masculine and feminine."

I certainly do *not* mean to suggest here that Latifah is a lesbian. I neither know nor seek the answer to that question. It is not even necessarily relevant that Latifah does not wish to characterize herself as a feminist. As she has explained: "I'm inclined to show women in as positive a light as I can. . . . A lot of people call me a feminist because of that, but I prefer the term common-sensist."[7]

Rather, I'm interested here in Latifah's refusal of monolithic definitions of "female" experience and desire. This refusal, I would say, plays an important role in shaping gender representation (and reception) in *Living Single.* In the next part of this chapter, then, I want to look closely at Latifah's pre–*Living Single* productions, both as a rapper and as a feature film actor.

Beginning with *All Hail the Queen,* her 1989 debut album, we find what cultural theorist Tricia Rose describes as a strong statement for "black female unity, independence, and power."[8]

As a rapper, Latifah was part of a network of female performers (including MC Lyte, Monie Love, and Yo-Yo) who addressed both male chauvinism and racism in their personal lives as well as in their music. In fact, the political activism of Yo-Yo (who later landed a recurrent role on *Martin*) led to the founding of what she called the Intelligent Black Women's Coalition, a support network "for sisters of all races" dedicated to "increasing the status and self-esteem of all women."[9] It is important to note that Latifah was strongly associated with the collective work of black women rappers and activists.

Next we come to Latifah's feature role in the 1991 film *House Party 2.* Here the actor plays Zora, a dashiki-wearing feminist activist and African American studies major named after 1930s author and anthropologist Zora Neale Hurston. In a delightful twist of intertextuality, Latifah's character becomes both roommate and mentor to a starry-eyed young student named Sydney, played by an extremely young-looking Tisha Campbell.

If Khadijah James of *Living Single* could have rapped to Gina Waters of *Martin,* their conversation might have resembled Sydney and Zora's first meeting. Settling into her new dorm room, Sydney holds up a bit of lingerie and asks: "Isn't it cute?" Zora's reply is icy. "When I first got here," she warns, "I had a drawer *full* of little boy-toy frou-frous just like that. . . . But I grew up and let my consciousness evolve. And when I left all that male materialism behind, I began to see things in a more politically correct light."

"You *do* like boys, don't you?" demands Sydney, her eyes suddenly growing wide. "I like men," replies Zora. "But I don't need one to define me. And any woman who wants to define herself . . . has to free herself of all that tired, lame male bullshit" ("bullshit" being the frou-frou lingerie). With that, Sydney's boyfriend, played by the rapper Kid, appears armed with a rainbow strip of condoms. "Pick a color," he urges Sydney. "Male bullshit," adds Zora, exiting in a huff.

Thanks to Zora's influence, Sydney undergoes dramatic changes during her first year at college. She begins to wear headscarfs and kente cloth and, much to Kid's dismay, even replaces a course entitled Afro-American Consciousness of the Sixties (which examines James Baldwin, Ralph Ellison, Richard Wright, and the theme of growing up as a black male in America) with one recommended by Zora—Male Mythology: A Feminist Perspective.

A particularly interesting scene takes place at a rally against ethnic studies cutbacks. At the protest, Zora the activist makes a rousing speech and, in a fascinating insertion of Latifah, inspires her cohorts with a song. What's intriguing about this performance is the lyrics. Although the setting is an ethnic studies rally and not a specifically feminist one, Zora's song focuses on sexual harassment on the job, which she then refers to, oddly enough, as "racism."

This unlikely confluence—of ethnic studies, racism, and sexual harassment—is indicative of the profound subtextual tension embodied in Latifah's persona: that is, the tension between race and gender, and the struggle to reconcile feminist and nationalist desires.[10] In Spike Lee's 1991 *Jungle Fever,* for example, Latifah plays a regally clad waitress hostile to the notion of interracial dating. The nationalist aesthetics of *Living Single* also expressed a certain racial pride, symbolized by books such as *African Americans: Voices of Triumph* and *I Dream A World,* strewn across the coffee table, Africanesque statues placed throughout the living room, kente fabrics hanging from a coatrack, and baseball caps reading "Negro League." This aesthetic was not presented *in opposition* to feminist desire; rather, the two coexisted.

Returning to the conclusion of *House Party 2,* Zora takes an unconventionally "masculine" stance. When an abusive suitor attempts to woo Sydney, Zora inserts her own body to prevent them from touching. And although it is Kid who eventually rescues Sydney from sexual assault, Zora has a hand in saving the day by delivering a right jab to the con artist who stole Kid's scholarship funds (played by supermodel Iman).

In *Living Single,* it becomes clear that Latifah brings these extratextual personas with her. In one storyline, for example, a male acquaintance refers to Regine as a "bitch." At the end of the episode, there is a music video tag scene in which Latifah performs her 1994 testament against sexism, "U.N.I.T.Y." As she told a reporter when her single went gold: "I'm clearly not the only one tired of hearing black women being referred to as bitches and ho's."[11]

In the tag scene, Naughty By Nature's Treach (Anthony Criss) physically assaults Latifah by grabbing her ass as she walks down the street. In response, Latifah spins around to confront him—"Who you calling a bitch?"—just before throwing a punch. This tag scene performs a unique ideological function within the

Living Single episode, effectively recruiting the feminist persona of Latifah (donning dark shades and black leather, no less) to respond to the fictional Regine's objectification.

Finally, I want to look at Latifah's most controversial and critically acclaimed role: as Cleo in F. Gary Gray's 1996 feature film *Set It Off.* In the action drama, Latifah plays a hot-blooded, tequila-drinking, ganja-smoking woman from the 'hood who decides, with three of her girlfriends, to rob a bank. Cleo, as Latifah explains, is "a straight-up dyke . . . men's drawers, the whole nine."[12] In one particularly memorable scene, Cleo shares her loot with her svelte, blond-Afroed girlfriend, Ursula (Samantha MacLachlan). As the scantily clad Ursula dances seductively above her, Cleo caresses and kisses her thigh. Latifah acknowledged the role was a daring one—not only because she tongue-kisses a woman on camera, but because, as *Vibe* writer Danyel Smith noted, "she does it so well."

And yet, more than two years after the release of *Set It Off,* the nation's most venerated rap magazine, *The Source,* continued to entertain the question—"Wassup with dat gay stuff anyway?" as writer Amy Linden put it—in a lengthy six page cover story on Latifah.[13] The fuel for this most recent fire was provided by the rapper's own 1998 CD, *Order In the Court,* or rather, by two missing songs found only on an underground mix tape sampler. "Nigga get off my dick," she raps, "and tell your bitch to come here."

When asked about the lyrics by *The Source,* Latifah spends a great deal of time discussing intimate details of her sexual past, likes and dislikes, and yet she refuses to address directly the question of lesbianism. This is precisely what Christina Lane means, I think, when she refers to the "space of unknowing" that serves to disalign Foster, and in this case Latifah, from static definitions of female sexuality. "I wanted to drop something hard," notes the rapper, "something hot. I wanted to rhyme without worrying about what I said."

"Latifah knows there are people who question her own sexuality," writes Smith. "Folks make a parlor game of trying to find homoerotic subtexts in the heterocentric *Living Single.*" But *Set It Off* director F. Gary Gray is dismissive of the is-she-or-isn't-she question that swirls around Latifah. "Latifah is different from Cleo; Cleo is different from Khadijah; Khadijah is different from Dana [Owens, Latifah's given name]."

In looking at Latifah's various on-screen roles, then, we see that her feminist and lesbian characterizations represent an integral part of her overall persona as a popular icon among African American audiences. Moreover, because she is situated within a community of hip-hop artists, a whole body of narrative possibilities is linked to her characterizations—possibilities that both challenge patriarchal contexts and affirm a kind of womanist Africanity. Latifah's sexual liminality is present not only in fictional television and film but also in her documentary or real-life persona.

In a 1991 interview for *Essence* magazine, writer Deborah Gregory gushes over Latifah's newfound attraction to eyeliner, lipstick, and acrylic nail tips, concluding that Latifah proves "female rappers can look like real women too." In contrast, Latifah squashes that angle by saying that despite her "feminine additions," she will never become "the ultrafem kind of girl who's scared of knocking one hair out of place."[14]

In another 1993 interview, this time for *Ebony,* Latifah's "masculine" look is again noted, as writer Aldore Collier describes her appearance in overalls, hiking boots, and a sweatshirt. After the workday is over, notes Collier, Latifah "grabs a helmet, tosses her sandy hair, jumps on her motorcycle and zooms off." When Collier asks the actor about the matter of her dress, Latifah responds with this: "Some girls would not wear this at all. They would feel boyish. I feel comfortable and I wear what I like. Some people place femininity on the exterior, but it's inside."[15]

In conclusion, I propose that black female autobiography and authorship, as well as strong feminist (even lesbian) tendencies, are evident throughout *Living Single.* This comes about not only through the powerful fictional, presentational, and documentary personas of Latifah, but also through the show's overt story lines. For example, one episode depicts a lesbian marriage between an old college roommate of Max's and her lover. Interestingly, Regine, Synclaire, and Maxine all react to news of the wedding in ways that are either inappropriate or hostile. Khadijah, however, manages to stroll through the proceedings unperturbed.

We might say that this popular icon, this Dana-Latifah-Zora-Cleo-Khadijah figure serves as a meeting ground upon which gender and sexual battles can be negotiated. As Danyel Smith wrote of Latifah's *Set It Off* character: "Cleo is not some boilerplate bulldagger. She's a full-blown human with issues that have roots in the black part, the poor part, the woman part, and the provincial part." Now that's more like it: a woman of intrigue, whose sexuality represents only part of her total black, womanist self.

Part 3

Social Movement

"This is a journey, we discover, primarily toward our own selves.
A journey to discover who we still are,
after all these years of the most devastating humiliation,
subjugation, enslavement, and eradication . . .

Art unfailingly reflects its creator's heart. Art that comes from
a heart open to all the possible paths
there might be to a healthier tomorrow cannot help
but be medicine for the tribe."

From Anything We Love Can Be Saved,
by Alice Walker

6

Under the Sign of Malcolm: Memory, Feminism, and Political Activism on Roc

Hoping to portray a family experience more complex and representative than *Cosby*'s picture-perfect lifestyle, Charles Dutton, executive producer and star of *Roc,* set out to portray a working-class black family with all the love and devotion of the Huxtables, minus the wealth. His show revolved around Roc Emerson, an honest and hardworking employee of the Baltimore sanitation department (a "garbage engineer," as he says), and his wife Eleanor (Ella Joyce), a nurse. While saving for their dream home, the Emersons share a brownstone with Roc's errant brother, Joey (Rocky Carroll), and curmudgeonly father, Andrew (Carl Gordon).

The ensemble cast was already familiar to some viewers; the actors had earned critical acclaim for their collective performance in August Wilson's stage hit *The Piano Lesson.* When Dutton got the call from Fox to do a television show, he packed up his co-stars and brought them with him. This is important. Because the vast majority of *Roc*'s creative team—its writers, producers, cast members, and even one executive—were single-mindedly committed to the social vision of Charles Dutton (whose real-life nickname is "Roc"), this staff was unusually coherent in both its goals and sensibilities.

Key members of the production team also included staff writers Vince Cheung and Ben Montanio, who referred to themselves as "rice and beans" in homage to their Chinese and Mexican-American heritages; actor Franklin Ajaye (*Car Wash*), who came on board as a writer following an unsuccessful stint on *In Living Color;* and Stan Lathan, perhaps black television's most prominent director.[1]

In addition, *Roc* was unusual in that its production supervisor on the executive side was also African American, at a time when few, if any, black executives oversaw prime-time network shows. As director of HBO Independent Productions (HIP), Kyle Bowser (supervising producer on both *Roc* and *Martin*) was actually the first black programming executive ever to be hired by HBO, and his presence was crucial. Not only did he serve as a mediator between network executives and creative talent, but the young attorney was an instigator in his own right.

Because of like-minded politics and sensibilities among *Roc*'s creative team, then, the group was able to produce, on a surprisingly consistent basis, collective autobiography and intraracial dialogue. Unlike the chaos of *The Sinbad Show* or the megalomania of *Martin,* there was a genuine sense of cohesion on this show, in which mostly African American creators fought tooth and nail for their collective visions.

This is not to say that *Roc*'s staff escaped ideological struggles with Fox or other HBO executives. It certainly did not. In fact, the battles waged and lost by the crew often took the form of sly stylistic and casting changes instituted by the network. These are fascinating case studies, because while *Roc*'s team may have objected adamantly to such modifications, viewers were unlikely to have even noticed them, so subtle were the shifts.

An example of one such change involved the show's title sequence and theme song. During the first two seasons, a mournful rendition of "God Bless the Child" sung a cappella by the Persuasions played against chiaroscuro panshots of Baltimore streets. In conjunction with this opening, audiences were introduced to the dramedy through gritty shots of liquor stores, check-cashing establishments, and city buses. In *Roc*'s third season, however, the opening sequence underwent a striking makeover. Viewers were now treated to an upbeat R&B theme performed by glamour-girl pop vocalists En Vogue. In the title sequence's new incarnation, *Roc*'s urban streets were replaced by sunburst graphics and cheery smiles all around.

A second modification was the elimination of Roc's co-workers. Whereas in earlier seasons Roc was often seen talking shop in the Sanitation Department locker room, in later episodes, he was no longer seen working at all. Instead, he now spent his leisure time in a local bar. Just as the Ujamaa coop in *South Central* provided a setting for exploring nationalist desire, the locker room would have been clearly more conducive to story lines involving issues of workers' rights, solidarity, and/or social justice.

Other battles were completely removed from viewers, such as the one fought by Kyle Bowser over a 1992 election-year episode. As this script was originally written, Roc was to be upset by the fact that political candidates always fail to fulfill promises related to "low wages, homelessness, and urban violence." Frustrated and disillusioned, Roc refuses to vote. While supportive of the episode's overall theme, Bowser was bothered by its conclusion, which had Roc suddenly deciding to vote for no reason other than narrative closure.

To make the finale more plausible, Bowser invited the Reverend Jesse Jackson to inspire Roc via a televised speech. Though Jackson agreed to the appearance, as did most Fox executives, the revised script was shot down by executive producer Jeff Abugov, who suggested that Jackson appear on a future episode with a different theme. Shortly afterward, Bowser expressed his concerns in a "state of the series" memo to Fox, in which he noted a "general insensitivity to issues being raised by Dutton's creative team." In response, Bowser received a late-night phone call from a network supervisor who wanted to know if he was "some kind of militant."

Similar struggles abounded throughout *Roc*'s tenure, but there was one that Dutton vowed to win: the battle for drama.[2] In the next section of this chapter I look at three dramatic episodes from the show's final season—episodes that some say were the cause of *Roc*'s downfall.

In addition to the sitcom's "hip" new graphics and R&B theme song, viewers were also introduced to a new cast member in the 1993–94 season: an adopted teenager named Sheila Hendricks (Alexis Fields) who, like the Huxtables' cousin Pam, was brought on to help the network target a younger demographic.

In the first episode of what would become a dramatic trilogy, we meet Terence Lambert (Brandon Adams), a school friend of Sheila's. From the start, viewers are led to believe that Terence is a "good" boy. We know this because his grandfather was a fellow sanitation worker whom Roc knew and admired, and because Terence demonstrates upstanding, middle-America values. "No sex is the safest sex," he tells an approving Roc.

Despite his apple-pie upbringing, however, we soon learn that Terence has been "packing" a gun to defend himself against gang members at school. Discovering the weapon, Roc demands an explanation. "Mr. Emerson, it's not like when you were a kid," begins Terence. "I can't just duke it out with this guy on the playground. If you wanna stand up for yourself today, you gotta be strapped." Roc eventually convinces Terence to give up the gun, of course. And to show there are no hard feelings, he even gives the boy a few dollars to buy some ice cream. But it's too late. Seconds after Terence steps outside the Emerson home, his young body is riddled with bullets.

The most striking aspect of this episode is its refusal of comedy. Beginning with the drive-by shooting of Terence, the narrative absolutely abandons the sitcom format to present fifteen minutes of hardcore drama. In the following scenes, prolonged silences punctuate long shots of the grief-stricken family. There are moments when the only sound is Sheila's muffled cries.

Finally Eleanor speaks: "Roc. What is happening in this city?" After four long beats Roc replies, "I don't know, baby." Two beats. "I don't know." Fade to black.

Immediately afterward we fade in to a classroom where Roc/ Dutton faces the camera directly and delivers an unconventional monologue. As he "breaks the fourth wall" to speak directly to viewers (just as Andre/Larenz Tate did in his *South Central* tag speech), the camera pulls back to reveal a roomful of teenagers. His partially improvised speech, which ran over two minutes on air and ended in a fade to black, is worth citing in full.

> How many kids have to kill each other before we see? There have already been thousands. Thousands of beautiful, gifted kids whose lives are over. There will be no future for them. No tomorrow. All their great potential is wasted forever. These are our own kids, killing each other. Our own kids are doing what three hundred years of slavery couldn't do, what the Ku Klux Klan couldn't do, and what all the ugly racism we faced for generations couldn't do. They're threatening our spirit, breaking our hearts, and destroying us from within. Now, Martin Luther King didn't die for that. Not to see our own children threatening the survival of our people. Malcolm X didn't die for that. Now, I know how hard it is out there. I know how hopeless it feels . . . the epidemic of drugs, the lack of jobs, the deprivation and killing in our community, and almost—and it *seems* like almost—nothing is being done about it. I know that. But killing ourselves is not the answer. And parents, we must take responsibility. You know, we have to take our children back and gain control. It is our individual responsibility to do this, to get our children back. We cannot let this slaughter continue. We gotta go on together and we have to live to realize the promise of our great struggle for all of us. . . . If you or someone you love has been a victim of a violent crime and need information, you call the national victim center at 1-800-FYI-CALL, and if you need help immediately call the Covenant House "Nine Line" at 1-800-999-9999. Let's end the violence in our community and among our youth.

It's important to note the slippages in Dutton's speech. When Dutton changes his line from "almost nothing is being done" to "it *seems* like almost nothing is being done," the text reveals an important ideological shift—a tenuous conservatism, which reappears in the following episode.[3]

In the second part of this trilogy, Dutton's team again defies the sitcom norm by refusing to begin with a new or unrelated story line. Instead, Roc calls for a community meeting to address recent violence in the neighborhood. After some discussion among the attendees, it is decided that Roc should run for city council. Again, we should note the ways in which his fictional monologue mirrors that of the previous episode's presentational speech:

> Before I tell you about my platform, I'd like to talk to you about why I'm running. A couple of weeks ago, a twelve-year-old boy was gunned down in cold blood on my front steps. Terence Lambert. Terence was a good kid. He was a good student. He came from a good family. Terence was killed by a gang member. Another kid. Over a jacket. Now, Terence was not the first boy to die in our neighborhood, and he won't be the last. Because these dealers and these gangs are either shooting each other or killing themselves with drugs. We can't wait for someone else to fix this. We've gotta fix it ourselves. . . . It's up to the people of this community to take personal responsibility to clean this neighborhood up.[4]

Audiences familiar with *Roc*'s earlier seasons may remember the prevalence of Malcolm X imagery in the Emerson home—portraits of Malcolm X that were hung on the family's walls by Andrew Emerson. By the 1993–94 season, however, director Stan Lathan had began to deemphasize these shots. They had become "overdone," Lathan told me, and had simply begun to "bore" him. Instead, Malcolm X imagery was replaced with, for example, shots of Africanesque fabrics draped on the walls—a shift more significant than I suspect Lathan realizes. Rather than framing hopes of justice around a single, heroic figure, the fabric imagery (used as a backdrop in one of Roc's election speeches) connotes the distinct possibility of a collective *social movement.*

Another exciting element here is that Roc's campaign begins as a multicultural alliance. Schoolteacher Carlos (Luis Antonio Ramos) is a friend of Roc's who becomes a core member of the campaign team. Functioning as a link between Roc and the Latino Voting Committee, Carlos describes Latino support for Roc in colloquial "Spanglish": "They threw a lot of tough questions at him, *pero* he was right there with all the answers. I think we got an awful lot of votes, because at the end they were all shouting, '*Adelante,* Roc.'"

At the taping for this episode I was also struck by a close-up of Carlos, who crosses himself at the mention of Terence's name. If black television poses questions such as "Whom shall we call family?" and "Where shall we find safe spaces?" then episodes such as this one provide refreshing answers. Alliances among African Americans and Latinos are neither given nor inherent here. Rather, they are hard-won, cherished, and entirely possible. The moment vanishes quickly, though: the shot of Carlos mourning Terence is not included in the episode's final edit.

Instead, the text concludes by shying away from such bold alliances, and returns us to a relatively narrow space of resistance, in which the Nation of Islam becomes *the* site of black liberation. While the Nation of Islam is certainly a primary source of community activism in the war against drugs, as Angela Davis has written, it often forecloses alliances with non-black people of color, gay and lesbian activists, feminists, and progressive whites.[5] Instead, the Nation of Islam returns us to essentialist notions of blackness—a move that is particularly disappointing in the final episode of this trilogy.

In the third episode, Joey (now Roc's campaign manager) fills the house with miniskirted, light-skinned "volunteers" assigned to lick envelopes and answer phones. These women have no function beyond being attractive, and in fact do not ever speak. Even Eleanor, who initially plays the role of helpmate in her husband's campaign, quickly folds into being a silent mother and wife. When druglord Andre Thompson (played by Clifton

Powell, who would later become the Afrocentric Bobby Deavers in *South Central*) appears at her door, Eleanor retreats, allowing her husband to take over.

As the story line goes, Thompson wants Roc out of the race. Roc refuses. Threats are exchanged and male bravado is displayed. Interestingly, this is where both Carlos and the women disappear. Instead, Joey quickly organizes a group of neighborhood men to confront Thompson. His collective includes William Long (Bodja Djola), who runs a gambling ring; a Nation of Islam member who vows that "with the help of Allah we will get the drugs out of this neighborhood"; and Ronnie Paxton, a neighborhood cab driver played by rapper Tone Loc.

Tone Loc's presence here is particularly rich. Entering the narrative with virtually no contextual explanation, his character is necessarily derived from the rapper's documentary, presentational, and fictional personas. Moreover, his striking aesthetic shifts within this episode—sudden changes in clothing and manner—position audiences differently according to the needs of each scene.

For example, when Loc initially appears in the Emerson home, he wears a black sweatshirt bearing the image of a face split down the middle, with one side brown and one side white, a chain of bondage around the neck, and the words "Man of Africa" below.[6] When Ronnie Paxton addresses Andre Thompson, however, he wears dark sunglasses and a knit cap, and his diction and mannerisms differ from elsewhere in the episode. "Let me tell you something right now, Dre," he warns. "Something funna [a blackism that combines "fixing to" and "gonna"] change in this community right now, whether you like it or not." Viewers familiar with Tone Loc's documentary activities (namely, his participation in the 1990 Stop the Violence Movement) will read even more layers of meaning into the moment.

In the final scene we're returned to the Emerson home, where Ronnie is now a mere neighborhood visitor among many. Wearing a plain button-down shirt, his clothing and manner are indistinguishable from those of other community members.

Through this shifting signification of Tone Loc (rapper, Man of Africa, and average-Joe neighbor) the narrative links itself both to middle-class values, exemplified by Roc Emerson's sliding conservatism, and to the self-help philosophy of the Nation of Islam, as well as to members of hip-hop communities.

The episode concludes with an optimistic speech by Roc. "We didn't lose this campaign," he tells his supporters. "We won. It's a victory that Easterwood Park is safe for the kids again! Look, we built an organization that can turn this neighborhood around. I don't have to be a councilman for us to demand safer neighborhoods, better schools, and parks where our children can play. This is *our* government. We should stay in their faces until they listen." Unfortunately, who "our" represents is now unclear. Whereas the narrative flirts with the notion of multiracial coalition, it is ultimately returned to patriarchal nationalism and a narrow, "black" unity.

It may well be that this trilogy of interrelated episodes was the proverbial straw that broke the Fox's back.[7] It's far more likely, however, that the network had already decided not to renew the show. In either case, Dutton's manipulation of the sitcom genre created a great deal of tension at the network. As *Roc* Supervising Producer Richard Dubin noted at the time: "Fox is not real comfortable with us being as direct about issues as we are. I work very closely with Charles, so I'm not someone they would come to with 'Shit, these niggahs are out of hand,' but I can imagine that they've wrung their hands in the company of others with that kind of feeling."

Relations between *Roc*'s creative team and Fox certainly were strained, agreed director Stan Lathan (who also had a producer credit on the show). As with *South Central,* the network thought of the show as a sitcom, explained Lathan. "Charles didn't like that term for his show, and that's where there seemed to be a clash of philosophies. . . . Charles's feelings were a little bit out of sync with what Fox wanted to present."

In the final section of this chapter, I look at an episode of *Roc* that seems to applaud black feminist struggle. The episode (called "R-E-S-P-E-C-T") begins with Roc, Joey, and their friend Sly (Darryl Sivad) watching football in the Emerson living room. Overhearing their crude sexual comments about the cheerleaders, Eleanor expresses her disappointment to Roc. This conversation sets up the central story line, which is that Sly's son, Stevie (Wayne Collins Jr.), has been sexually harrassing Sheila at school.

The question of authorship is interesting here in that the episode was written by a black woman, Alison Taylor. There are moments in which the text supports a specifically black feminist consciousness and worldview. Some of these moments are consciously scripted; others are not. In one scene, for example, Joey is criticized for living off his brother and pregnant sister-in-law—who, it is noted, "waits on him hand and foot." Another moment occurs when Eleanor tells Sheila, "If us women would just stick together as sisters . . . we could rule the world."

Within this consciously feminist context, however, there is also a fascinating moment that is unscripted and subtextual—and which has more to do with the set design, camera angles, and stage movements than actual dialogue. The scene begins with a parent-teacher meeting to discuss the conflict between Sheila and Stevie. As we open, Sheila is seated alone on one side of a classroom. Stevie and his father are across the room. Soon Eleanor and Roc enter from the door nearest Sheila, followed by an African American female teacher, who enters from a door midway between the two groups. Directly behind Eleanor, Roc, and Sheila are vague glimpses of historical text and photos, and a banner that reads "Black Americans."

What is striking is that these photos remain blurred throughout most of the scene. In fact, it is not until the precise moment in which the word *feminist* is uttered for the first time that the images become clear. When the teacher asks for Roc's opinion about the situation, he starts to say that Sheila has been influenced by some "feminist [thought]." At that exact moment, he shifts his stance and the figures on the wall are seen clearly.

Not only are they photos of black Americans, as the banner reads, but more specifically, they're photos of the black American freedom fighters Harriet Tubman and Sojourner Truth.

What these aesthetics accomplish is an ideological reframing of the debate itself, recontextualizing "unwanted compliments" as part of an ongoing legacy of womanist resistance. When the teacher asks Stevie to "tell his story," on the other hand, both father and son are framed by an image of Malcolm X on the classroom wall, symmetrically situated just above Stevie's head. This trinity is separated from the rest of the room by an open door frame, which draws a dividing line between the two groups. When Stevie insists that he was only offering "compliments," Sheila moves closer to the historical documentation on the wall—closer to Tubman and Truth.

"This isn't just about compliments," she explains. "He told me I looked real sexy in my top. And when I told him to go away, he started singing this song to me . . . the kind that call girls bitches and ho's. And when I turned to walk away from him, he grabbed my butt. That's when I hit him." At this point, Sheila defies the boundary between herself and the trinity imagery by lunging toward Stevie, who moves to hide behind his father. This repositioning is fascinating in that Sheila now occupies Stevie's position directly under the image of Malcolm, and side by side with the father. Although she remains here only briefly, the transgression is profound as it disrupts the privileging of male desire as "black history."

In general, then, *Roc* sought to reimagine monolithic formulations of the black family, home, and community. At times its narratives retreated back into narrow paradigms of social movement, such as the Nation of Islam; restrictive iconography, such as the redundant Malcolm X imagery; and even conservative black nationalism and self-help philosophies. At other times, however, the text transcended such frameworks brilliantly, bursting forth with fresh possibilities for grassroots coalitions, feminist movements, and racial and economic justice.

7
Boricua Power in the Boogie-Down Bronx: Puerto Rican Nationalism on New York Undercover

New York Undercover was the number one show among African Americans from 1994 to 1996.[1] Why? Or perhaps a better question is: What happened from 1996 to 1998? Why did it change? In its first season, mainstream television critics pointed to the macho good looks of actors Malik Yoba and Michael DeLorenzo as the key to *Undercover*'s success. Some noted that the funky beats inspired by former producer and music executive Andre Harrell also played a part in attracting young viewers. These factors, while important, provided only a superficial analysis of the show's appeal. It was, in fact, the dynamic interplay of drama, collective autobiography, improvisation, and aesthetics that made this show a hit.

New York Undercover was the first prime-time dramatic series to star *both* an African American and a Latino as lead characters. If we consider it a "black" drama, it was also the first ever to succeed past season one. The show has its origins in the research of African American writer-producer Kevin Arcadie, who modeled *Undercover*'s twenty-something detectives, J. C. Williams (Yoba) and Eduardo Torres (DeLorenzo) after three real-life rapping cops from Chicago known as the "Slick Boys."

Although the series was compared to its predecessors, *Miami Vice* (which also employed *Undercover*'s executive producer, Dick Wolf, from 1986 to 1988) and *Miami Undercover*, a 1961 syndicated crime drama, this hip-hop incarnation was not based on a black-white buddy premise. Rather, it delved deep inside the cultural nuances, biases, fears, and desires of its African American and Latino characters and audiences. What captivated in-group viewers most, I propose, was *Undercover*'s rich interpretations of family, loyalty, and collective responsibility to *la raza* (translated literally as "the race" and used to express shared Latino allegiances).

Once again, the question of authorship is a tricky one here. Although *Undercover* was shaped by African American influences, ultimate control of the series remained in the hands of Dick Wolf (*Law and Order*), its white executive producer who shared a "created by" credit with Kevin Arcadie. Also on Wolf's creative team were Andre Harrell, writers Reggie Rock Bythewood and Charles Holland, and post-production editor ("the final rewrite") Arthur Forney, all of whom were black. How much decision-making power these men had, individually or collectively, depends on whom you ask."It was a show that came out of a black experience," recalled Arcadie. "Andre Harrell brought the music and the single-father issue. I brought the flavor and point of view. . . . The secret to the show was its [black] attitude."

"I was on *A Different World* for two years," noted Bythewood. "And every episode there was issue, issue, issue. I don't think that's the case here, but [occasionally] we do get to deal with some important themes." Bythewood once wrote a script about a cigarette company that targeted minorities in its advertising campaigns, for example. Fox thought the issue too volatile. But because Dick Wolf fought for it, says Bythewood, the episode was aired.

Kevin Arcadie recalled *Undercover*'s power dynamics differently, saying, "I consider it a victory that for the first nine episodes of *Undercover* the writers were basically left on their own." Because Wolf was initially working on other projects, his time was divided, said Arcadie. This changed however, when Fox ordered a full season of episodes for 1994. "The only way you could get the network's respect was if Dick [defended you]," explained Arcadie. "Which he never did." According to Arcadie, a white "mystery writer" named Bob Ward was soon hired as supervising producer. It was a position many felt should have been offered to Arcadie, noted Rose Catherine Pinkney, who was vice president of television for Uptown Entertainment from 1993 to 1995.

And so began the gradual changes to *Undercover*'s authorship that would take place over the next four years. In 1994, during the show's first season, the writing staff was almost entirely African American and Latino. In 1995, neither Charles Holland nor Kevin Arcadie returned, leaving just three minority writers on a staff of seven (Judith McCreary and Reggie Bythewood, who are African American, and Natalie Chaidez, who is Mexican American). Although Andre Harrell's name remained officially tied to the show, his involvement was dramtically curtailed after the first season as well.[2]

Simply put, the series would most likely never have survived without Dick Wolf's powerful backing. With his cooperation, however, Fox eventually succeeded in making the show less "black." From the beginning, the network wanted radical changes to its premise. Executives even protested the concept of African American and Latino partners. "You're sure one of them can't be white?" they asked Wolf shortly after buying the show.

To say that black authorship existed and even thrived for a time, then, is not to say that the show's creative team was without cultural conflicts. Neither Bill Duke, who directed the pilot, nor Andre Harrell seemed happy with their experiences upon leaving. And although neither was willing to discuss the details of his displeasure for the record, it was clear that their interactions on the set had been tense.

Nevertheless, to the extent that Dick Wolf was receptive to African American and Latino creative input—particularly in the show's early days—*Undercover* had all the signs of a black production: a desire for dramatic representation, collective autobiography, aesthetics, and improvisation. As with other productions, these elements were usually interwoven.

For example, its aesthetics were deeply tied to collective black autobiography. Because Andre Harrell was president and founder of Uptown Entertainment when he signed on to do *Undercover*, artists such as Mary J. Blige, Montell Jordan, Brandy, Al B. Sure, Jodeci, Guy, and Heavy D and the Boyz became built-in musical backdrops for the show's nightclub scenes. As a result, the look of *Undercover* was "ultra-urban" and, to use one critic's words, "aggressively inner-city." In one scene, for example, would-be gang members cruise down New York streets to the beat of Grandmaster Flash's "The Message." In another, the lyrics of Tupac Shakur's "Dear Mama" accent sunfilled shots of desolate rooftops and urban decay.

Improvisation also had a function similar to the one it had in *The Fresh Prince of Bel Air*, where Will Smith altered scripted dialogue to make it more authentic. Throughout their respective tenures on the show, both Michael DeLorenzo and Malik Yoba were known for adding "street language" and "flavor" to their scripts in order to give the show credibility among urban viewers—a practice that was confirmed in my interviews with both Yoba and Natalie Chaidez. (In a fascinating aside, a critic for *Buzz* magazine actually complained that such "secret codes" unfairly excluded white viewers—further evidence of how uncomfortable in-group conversations were for some.)[3]

In the next section of this chapter, I discuss *Undercover*'s critique of what might be called knee-jerk race unity, particularly as it relates to "Latinoness." In countless episodes, the narrative repeatedly warns against using brown skin as a gauge of good will. Blind race solidarity is for suckers, story lines suggest, and reactionary brotherhood is for fools. As J. C. Williams notes in one episode, "There comes a point when [black] loyalty turns into ignorance."

Throughout the show's first season in particular, audiences are repeatedly confronted with characters like Donald Brooks (played by Clarence Williams III), a corrupt thief posing as a Harlem philanthropist and community activist; because of his seeming "downness" with the people, he is assumed to be innocent. Detective Williams finds it particularly difficult to accept the possibility of Brooks's guilt. "You still can't believe he would kill a black child, huh?" demands Lieutenant Virginia Cooper (Patti D'Arbanville-Quinn). "It's easier to believe a white man would do it?" When Torres and Williams finally do take the criminal down, Williams makes a point of ripping the decorative kente cloth from his neck.[4]

I want to look, then, at the ways in which "blind race loyalty" is exposed and critiqued within the context of Latino experiences. To do this, I focus on two episodes: one in which Torres interacts with a woman from the barrio, and another in which he is forced to grapple with Puerto Rican nationalism and his own allegiances.

In the first episode, Williams and Torres are introduced to Wall Street financial analyst Juanita Telles (Saundra Santiago), a murder witness who has been receiving death threats at her Upper East Side apartment. Torres assigns round-the-clock protection and takes a personal interest in her safety. After all, they come from the same place; Telles used to go dancing at La Bamba, a nightspot in the "boogie-down Bronx," and Torres once worked there as security.

Throughout the first half of this episode, Juanita Telles is seen as a victim. The shooter, meanwhile, is a deranged, ex–Navy Seal who leaves voice-distorted messages on her answering machine: "Juanita, Juanita. My little rose in Spanish Harlem." Of course, when Williams finally convinces Torres that his friend is a prime suspect herself, Torres jumps to Telles's defense on the basis of their shared heritage and working-class background. "There is no way Juanita did this," he insists. "She fought all her life to get where she is. Why would she jeopardize it?" Counting on just such a response, Juanita plays the race and class cards: "People like you and me," she tells Torres, "we've had to overcome so much to get where we are."

In the end, however, it becomes clear that Juanita is not the poor-girl-made-good that Torres has assumed her to be. Abandoning her careful business suit and tasteful pearls, Telles's final scene reveals a savvy criminal decked out in a black leather miniskirt, armed and on her way to retrieve a stolen fortune in the Cayman Islands. Meanwhile, her white co-conspirator (the deranged ex-Seal) dies with his face oddly camouflaged in brown paint.

What complicates this narrative even further is the fact that white racism is challenged just as vigilantly as is knee-jerk race loyalty. For example, in one scene Telles and her white co-worker are seen jogging through Central Park. Three black males approach them menacingly, calling out sexual innuendo. The women jog away. The men follow. One man taps the white woman's shoulder from behind. Danger seems imminent—but the black man only wants to return the woman's lost pager. This scene rallies in-group viewers (particularly black men) against white racism. At the same time, the central story line challenges such a simplistic stance, as Torres learns that shared heritage does not guarantee solidarity.

In the second episode (my favorite) called "Los Macheteros," this theme is again explored and challenged. Here, the sign of America as "home" is problematized for black and brown people alike, as Puerto Rican nationalists terrorize New York to raise money for their independence movement.

The episode, written by Natalie Chaidez, opens on four masked men in black leather gear rolling out of a van with automatic rifles. The men spray an armored truck with bullets. As the scene is adjusted to slow motion, the truck's Asian American driver falls to the ground. Hard, funky rap lyrics are spoken in Spanish. The nationalists speed away with the cash.

What's fascinating here is that although this is only a short montage, the American flag is featured in no less than ten frames. When the truck driver is killed, there is a flag on his uniform. Another, on the van door, becomes a blur of red, white, and blue as the vehicle tears away. In later scenes, Torres wears a red, white, and blue Tommy Hilfiger jacket. Miniature flags sit atop both his and Williams's desks. And finally, there is both a miniature flag *and* a larger, wall-sized model in Lieutenant Cooper's office. The American flag not only assaults viewers with patriotism but, in the context of the narrative, it also asks what citizenship really means for black and brown people.[5]

Torres and Williams soon discover that the armored-car heist was no random theft, but an organized operation executed by Puerto Rican political activists known as "Los Macheteros." "They call what they're doing *la lucha,*" explains Torres, remembering how such groups used to distribute free toys in his neighborhood when he was a boy. "Yeah, well, independence may be their agenda, Detective," interjects the hard-nosed Lieutenant Cooper. "But they're criminals. They pulled off a bank robbery in 1984. Five million dollars. They used the money to bomb a marine facility in San Juan."

Before continuing with textual analysis of this episode, I think it's appropriate to offer a cursory glimpse of the historical perspective of Puerto Rican nationalists—the perspective of both Torres and the fictional Macheteros—though of course I do not claim to present all sides of the debate in this short space.

Although Puerto Rico enjoys a relatively high living standard by comparison to other places in Latin America, the majority of the island's 3.5 million residents live in poverty. Puerto Rico is officially a commonwealth of the United States and has been associated with the United States since 1898, when Spain "gave" it as war booty to America. Today, Puerto Rico is the world's busiest drug port. The words of Independent Party president Rubén Berríos state the nationalist case well:

> We're the last remaining colony practically the world over. . . . Some 60% of our families live off food coupons. 40% of our potential work force is [unemployed]. . . . Puerto Rico ranks first in the world in homicides. . . . What does this mean? This means that colonialism in Puerto Rico breeds unemployment, social discontent, exile. . . . The

> dependent relationship with the United States makes our nation incapable of utilizing its power in order to produce employment, in order to find our own place under the sun. And then in order for people not to revolt, the United States sends food coupons. This is no future for anybody. We need independence to survive.[6]

Autobiographically, this history was important for writer Natalie Chaidez, who describes her Mexican-American family history as highly politicized. "My mother is an activist," she explains. "She runs a program for children of incarcerated parents in Pasadena. My grandmother worked in unions. My aunt is a Chicano studies professor at East L.A. College . . . chair of the department. My other aunt is also an activist. She worked on shutting down liquor stores in South Central. I was raised by these women. So that was my agenda coming in. Reggie [Bythewood] and I both had high aspirations from the beginning. We felt a responsibility to do issue-oriented shows."

Returning to the text, then, a subtle but interesting shift takes place about midway through the episode: the American flags disappear. Instead, viewers are suddenly confronted with a barrage of Puerto Rican flags, situated at key moments in the narrative. At a local community meeting, Torres (now working undercover as an independence activist) is framed by a large Puerto Rican flag directly behind him. In addition, a movement leader stands before a Puerto Rican flag as she speaks from the podium. Directly behind her, a mural depicts a woman steering a plow. In the painting, workers hold still more Puerto Rican flags. The mural's inscription reads: "*Hasta La Victoria Siempre.*"

"Next week the Senate is voting to build another military installation in Puerto Rico," announces the speaker. ("*Que malo!*" protest community members.) "Boricuas cannot be involved in this imperialism," she continues. "We have to oppose this vote here in New York, because on the island they have no direct representation." As she speaks, Torres greets Raul Sanchez, a fellow *independentista: "Cómo te va, Boricua?" "Bien, bien. Todo bien."*

It should be noted that the frequent use of Spanish throughout this episode plays a crucial role among in-group audiences. Some viewers know, for example, that indigenous Puerto Ricans (Taínos), often refer to themselves as "borinqueñas(os)." Some viewers also know that the island was only later renamed Puerto Rico ("rich port") upon the arrival of Christopher Columbus in 1493. Puerto Ricans who continue to refer to themselves as "boricuas" are generally seen as honoring their "true" history, as well as resisting imperialist notions of "discovery" and ownership.

Although assigned to infiltrate the *independentistas,* Torres (whose grandfather was almost killed fighting for independence) soon becomes conflicted in his loyalties. "It's like George Washington two hundred years ago," he confides in Williams. "All they want is their own country." "Yeah, but was [your grandfather] robbing a bank?" asks J.C. "Or was he throwin' some tea in the harbor?" "He was carrying a sign that said '*Puerto Rico Libre,*'" responds Torres.

In the meantime, Torres's brother Jimmy, a Catholic priest, wants Torres to protect Luis Moreno (Peter Jay Fernandez), a black Puerto Rican factory owner who donates generously to the church. Torres immediately distrusts Moreno, whom he sees as a sleek capitalist; a "sell-out" who takes "blood money" for U.S. defense contracts and allows for the continued domination of Puerto Rico. Now the question of loyalty becomes even more tangled: Does Torres side with Los Macheteros, who would like to see Moreno dead? Or does he help his brother, Jimmy, who wants Torres to protect the businessman?

By placing Torres somewhere between his brother's conservatism and the politics of Los Macheteros, the narrative once again complicates simplistic allegiances. It also gives Moreno a surprisingly dignified voice: "If my money can influence the vote," explains the handsome factory owner, "it will mean thousands of jobs for Puerto Rico. And that's a hell of a lot more than these so-called *independentistas* have ever done." "What good is money if he's selling out the whole island?" protests Ed. "That's easy for you to say," counters J.C., "cuz your ass ain't down there starving to death." "See, that's ignorance for you," Torres spits back. "Four hundred years and Puerto Rico is still a colony!"

In the end, the viewer is offered no easy closure. Instead, a sunset shot of the Statue of Liberty reigns over a calm harbor. As blue skies melt into orange and red, a Latina performer sings at the detectives' nightclub hangout—something about "*un gran necio*" who's done her wrong. Finding his brother at the bar, Jimmy tries to make peace, explaining that with Moreno's contribution to the church, he'll finally be able to build a housing project for homeless children. "But until Puerto Rico is independent," insists Torres, "there will always be Macheteros."

The final scene of the episode sees the brothers standing over their *abuelo*'s tombstone (the one who was almost killed for holding a "Puerto Rico Libre" sign). As Ed and Jimmy place two single red carnations over the grave, we read: "Digoberto Ortiz, 1917–1963: *Hasta La Victoria Siempre.*"

Whether consciously or not, in-group dialogue was clearly nurtured on this show as many episodes became intriguing debates about African American and Latino experience, memory, and desire. "The issues for us a lot of times are just part of our every day," explained Bythewood. "My mother worked at Harlem Hospital, and she told me what went on there. So I did a whole [show] dealing with black health care."

Within these conversations, actors and writers often functioned as cultural interpreters for white producers and executives. "They might say, 'Let's hire a [Latina],'" explained Malik Yoba. "And go for what we might see as a 'typical' look. If it's L.A., it would probably be a Mexican-looking person. If it's New York, they would look for a Puerto Rican person. But what does that mean? Come on, now. All you gotta do is watch the World Cup to understand the spectrum that Latinos fall under. They're everything from blond hair and blue eyes to the darkest person of African descent. . . . So show the true spectrum."

I should make it clear, however, that such in-group differentiation was regarded as particularly inaccessible to mainstream audiences. As producer Susan Fales notes, a sitcom script she once wrote, called "Independence Day," was doomed in part because it addressed differences between Puerto Ricans and Cubans. "It was like saying 'ashy skin,'" she recalled. "It was too inside."

So Fox's politics remained as ambiguous as ever. While the network had no desire to lose its urban viewership, Rupert Murdoch also yearned to expand into a white, global market. Thus, the show's contradictory practices during its second, third, and fourth seasons. On one hand, Lauren Velez (*I Like It Like That*) was hired as Detective Nina Moreno, to secure the show's Latino viewership. And yet she was brought onboard with newcomer Jonathan La Paglia, who played Detective McNamara. Now Fox finally had the "white guy" it had wanted from the show's inception. The following season, Michael DeLorenzo was summarily fired.[7] For the series' fourth and final season Tommy Ford (*Martin*) joined the cast as Lieutenant Malcolm Barker, oddly enough, while story lines became decidedly less race specific.

At the heart of the matter was a dual-edged sword: *Undercover*'s minority-heavy cast and in-group story lines did not necessarily appeal to white audiences, particularly in foreign markets. And yet the network couldn't yet risk losing its bread-and-butter African American and Latino audiences at home. By the show's third season, Fox had arrived at a decision. Wolf was told to make *Undercover* less "ethnic" or it would be taken off the schedule. In the process of retooling, the musical director, James Mtume, was told to omit all rap music while writer Judith McCreary was informed that more white lead characters were needed to sell the show overseas.

"To me," recalled McCreary, "that was like saying that my face, my features, my culture, my people are abhorrent to the world. I was angry. And deeply, deeply hurt." Given the show's new direction, McCreary chose not to renew her contract and resigned, along with three other writers, in disgust. "This is some plantation shit," noted Malik Yoba. "People . . . tell you that you're not good enough. When they say *New York Undercover* is number one in black households and number one hundred eight in white households, that's what they're saying."

But Dick Wolf saw Fox's mandate less as a cultural affront, than as a sound business decision. "Was it my original crystal-clear vision?" he responded rhetorically when asked about the show's changes. "No. Was it the right decision for a network to make? Absolutely. We're not trying to abandon black audiences," he added. "We're trying to attract more white viewers. And if you see a gangster rap video teaser in the middle of Harlem, a lot of [white] channel surfers are going to say: 'Nah, not for me.'"[8] Despite (or perhaps, because of) the changes, *Undercover* was finally canceled in February of 1998.

"I'm really unclear about whether or not Fox knows what their identity is at the moment," noted Yvette Lee Bowser at the start of the 1997–98 season. From 1994 to 1996 Bowser's *Living Single* had alternated with *Undercover* for the number one position in black households. In 1997, however, it was abruptly canceled to make room for an interracial buddy comedy and then returned to the schedule just as suddenly a few months later. "I think they're trying to find a formula and an identity. Perhaps they've lost theirs a little bit along the way."

In short, *New York Undercover*, like other black shows of the 1990s, was full of in-group conversations. In episodes written and produced by African Americans and Latinos, minority characters both rejected and desired race loyalty, rejected and desired Americanness, and wrestled with their own unique brands of nationalist desire. For cultural theorists, such contradictory dynamics were hopeful, as they refused easy definitions of what blackness is or should be. *New York Undercover* continued this important work, with stories that guided us through complex labyrinths of race yearning and *solidaridad.*

Conclusion

"Did you ask Keenen," inquired director Bill Duke when I interviewed him in his Pacific Palisades home, "who has the rights to all those *In Living Color* reruns in Asia, and all over the world?" It was a good question, one I had not asked. Which brings us to the problem of media ownership.

In 1997 the Reverend Jesse Jackson was again on the heels of the media monsters, noting in his keynote address to the National Association of Minorities in Communication that minority media ownership had fallen by 15 percent over the past year alone.[1] At this rate, continued Jackson, there might be no remaining minority-owned stations by the year 2004. Without delving too far into the legalese of the Federal Communications Commission (FCC), I think it worthwhile to highlight some key events in recent telecommunications history—events that slipped past us while we debated the pros and cons of "positive" versus "negative" imagery.

Twenty years ago President Nixon initiated a tax certification policy to help minority entrepreneurs buy fairer shares of the broadcast media pie. The incentive allowed for station owners and cable system operators to defer taxes on capital gains should they sell to minority buyers. As a result of the initiative, more than three hundred broadcast properties were sold to minorities over the next seventeen years, raising the percentage of minority ownership from 0.5 percent to a far grander 3 percent.

In 1995, however, something strange happened: An "especially slick" congressional bill generated "almost overnight" by Texas Republican Bill Archer called for an end to the tax incentive.[2] To ensure the bill's speedy passage, it was tucked inside an initiative to provide significant health care deductions for self-employed taxpayers—legislation that Republicans knew President Clinton wanted to see passed.

Why the sudden urge to end such a long-standing provision (barring the simple possibility of anti–civil-rights backlash, of course)? The answer had everything to do with Rupert Murdoch, who sought to destroy a pending deal between his competitor, Viacom, and minority investor Frank Washington. The cancellation of the tax incentive did just that.[3] (Fox, on the other hand, managed to squeeze through its own minority investment deal: the $150 million sale of an Atlanta station to Qwest, a minority-controlled venture founded by Quincy Jones, Don Cornelius, Geraldo Rivera, and former pro football star Willie Davis.)

The irony in these events is that throughout the late 1980s and early 1990s, Rupert Murdoch not only found ways to profit from the cultural production and consumption practices of African Americans but he also manipulated, to the collective detriment of black people, governmental infrastructures designed to balance the racially distorted playing field of media ownership. When such infrastructures threatened to limit Murdoch's monopolistic domination, in other words, he simply had them removed.

In 1994, for example, Fox took advantage of tax breaks for minority-owned enterprises by sinking $20 million into Blackstar Communications so that the minority venture could expand from three to fourteen stations (of which Fox would own a 20 percent interest). No act of goodwill, this was a move designed to circumvent FCC ownership limits. At the time, broadcast groups were limited to owning no more than twelve stations, covering no more than 25 percent of the nation's homes. In contrast, the limit for minority-controlled groups was fourteen stations and 30 percent coverage. Perhaps Jason Elkins, CEO of New Vision Television, put it most succinctly: "Those of us in broadcasting would [all] like to own twenty stations. It may be that Fox has found a way to do it through minority ownership."[4]

I've provided these brief musings on ownership so that we might keep in mind the larger contexts of global capitalism, even as we interrogate specific shows. In an environment in which government and market forces are actively hostile to non-white media ownership, the possibilities for black authorship are tentative at best. In fact, any potential for intraracial dialogue and collective autobiography in television is clearly mediated, sporadic, and forever subject to market-driven goals.[5]

Having said this, I'd like to close with a look at the changing landscape of black programming since 1994—the year that Fox canceled four of its six black shows. In 1993 Rupert Murdoch purchased the broadcast rights to Sunday afternoon football for $1.58 billion. This was followed by a $500 million deal with New World Communications that allowed Fox to expand from six to twenty-two stations, and to reach some 40 percent of U.S. households by 1997. Both transactions signaled the dawning of a new era for the fourth network, which was no longer content with its own "ghettoization" (or what was referred to in kinder days as "narrowcasting"). Because the fourth network now set out to be a legitimate contender alongside ABC, CBS, and NBC, it needed more white viewers.[6]

But the programming designed to entice Fox's newfound white male audience—shows such as *Fortune Hunter, Hardball,* and *Wild Oats*—were a dismal failure with the imagined beer-guzzling sports audience. Sunday's post-NFL schedule was gutted twice before Fox executives decided to backtrack, adding more of *The Simpsons* to its Sunday lineup, plus new episodes of the Latino-oriented *House of Buggin',* starring John Leguizamo.

But then came a surprise. Both Warner Brothers (WB) and

United Paramount (UPN) launched the "fifth" and "sixth" networks in 1996, consciously replicating Fox's early strategies in order to cash in on what now appeared to be an abandoned market. As Fox's president of sales noted, "[The new networks] are trying to outfox Fox, using our success in going for the young [black] audience."[7]

Just as Fox employees were once recruited from the then-blackest network, NBC, new WB employees were snatched up from Fox. Suzanne Daniels, who helped to develop *Living Single*, became head of prime-time development at WB; Jaime Kellner became chief executive; Garth Ancier was again programming chief; and Bob Bibb and Louis Goldstein, who promoted Fox during its first two years, became marketing heads. "We are basically targeting the same old Fox demos," noted Bibb and Goldstein. "We want to convey the same attitude of hip."[8]

For their respective 1996–97 seasons, both WB and UPN aired a string of black-cast comedies. On WB, these included: *The Wayans Brothers, The Parent 'Hood* (starring *Hollywood Shuffle* director Robert Townsend), *The Jamie Foxx Show,* and *Lush Life,* a pilot from Yvette Lee Bowser, which was quickly canceled. In addition, WB picked up both *The Steve Harvey Show* and *Sister, Sister* following their cancellations on ABC.

Encouraged by the success of its *Moesha,* UPN also immersed itself in programming starring African Americans and Latinos. Among its new pilots were *Working Guy,* a sitcom about a black veteran adjusting to life on Wall Street; *American Family,* which tracked the goings on of an upwardly mobile Latino family; *Goode Behavior,* starring Sherman Helmsley as a con-artist father who moves in with his university dean son; *Sparks,* with Robin Givens; *Malcolm and Eddie;* and *Homeboys from Outer Space.* UPN also picked up the L.L. Cool J vehicle, *In the House,* following its cancellation on NBC.

Although it could be argued that black stars and producers also exercised significant creative control on each of these shows, the later productions never explored intraracial issues with the same seriousness of purpose as earlier shows discussed above. In contrast African American decision makers such as Townsend, Shawn and Marlon Wayans, Jamie Foxx, Steve Harvey, and Suzanne de Passe almost never ventured beyond standard sitcom formats and mainstream, aracial themes. It is important to understand then, that while there were some twenty-one shows with black lead characters in 1997 (as compared to eight in 1990), these new series carefully avoided in-group dialogue around issues of color, class, gender, and sexuality. Network executives, it seems, now realized that they could have black-looking shows without the hassle of black complexity.

In fact, when ABC canceled its "black" lineup in 1995—shows like *On Our Own, Me and the Boys,* and *Sister, Sister*—*Los Angeles Times* television writer Rick DuBrow asked an important question: Why were these cancellations any different from Fox's axing of African American shows two years earlier? Why was there no protest over the cancellation of such "positive" black comedies? I would argue that black viewers did not complain—or even notice—because we had never invested the same degree of hope in these productions. These were black-*cast* shows as opposed to black *productions.* The shows that black audiences have been most passionate about, historically, are those presenting African American characters as multilayered, historical subjects who are ever-conscious of the collective.[9]

At the time of this writing, Fox is still the top-rated network among African American and Latino audiences. But the new networks have taken a sizable chunk out of Murdoch's earnings, and it now seems that Fox is not yet ready to abandon so completely its race-specific programming. In 1997, for example, Fox president Peter Roth cut a deal with Damon Wayans to do two shows. Because Fox desperately wanted the former *In Living Color* star in a comedy, it agreed to air thirteen episodes of Wayans's pet project, the hard-hitting one-hour drama series, *413 Hope Street.*

The deal quickly went sour, however, when Wayans realized

that Fox had no real interest in black drama. The network invested little in its promotional campaign, placed the series in a suicide time slot, put it on hiatus for a month or so, and eventually yanked it altogether after airing only ten episodes.

While viewers aren't likely to see the Fox of the early 1990s again, racial narrowcasting remains an essential strategy for broadcast outlets such as Fox, WB, and UPN, as well as for cable stations such as Black Entertainment Television (BET), which purchased the rights to *Roc* and *Frank's Place* following their respective cancellations on network TV.[10] The growing Latino audience has also inspired Spanish-language premium services such as GEMS Television (the equivalent of Lifetime for Latinas), HBO en Espanol, and the Fox Latin American Network.

In short, the wave of the future for in-house, culturally specific dialogue will not necessarily be in network television. More and more, it will probably be found in cable or on-line services. As *Entertainment Weekly* speculated, "The bigger UPN and the WB get, the whiter they'll become."[11] Whatever possibilities the new technologies may present, authorship will continue to be mediated by increasingly consolidated, transnational media conglomerates. I think Keenen Ivory Wayans raised an important point when he challenged the very premise of this book. "Why does everyone go after Martin," he asked, "when Disney is a *worldwide* supplier to little girls?"

I'm not particularly optimistic about the future of African American cultural representation. As Wayans reminded me, "Fox changed the course of black television *unintentionally*. They didn't go out to make black shows. They went out to make alternative programming. And when I came along with *In Living Color*, they were actually very fearful of what I was doing. But they knew that it was something different. And that's what they have to get credit for. By allowing that voice to be expressed, they discovered a whole new audience." Like an unfaithful lover, Fox continues to need black viewers—but on its own terms.

"The only reason Fox, WB, and UPN get involved in black

programming," added a network vice president who did not wish to be named, "is so that they can temporarily sustain themselves. The minute they can, they pull out. The last thing these executives want to do is go to parties and talk about *Sparks, Sparks,* and more *Sparks.* It's something they want nothing to do with." "They build themselves up with black audiences," agreed former *New York Undercover* producer Judith McCreary. "Then once they're established, they dump us."

This book bears witness to the internal contradictions of African American producers and consumers. While our collective yearning for the mythical American dream is apparent in virtually every episode of every black-produced show, black Americans are stepping into a new century largely removed from the benefits of a global capitalist economy. Our challenge remains one of critical engagement. Because visual media colonize our imaginations, we must continue to strive for vigilant and sophisticated readings of television culture. We must continue to create transformative psychic—and physical—spaces in which to live fuller, more just lives.

Television, like the larger society it reflects, is at a crossroads. Shall we live and work and play together, or not? Integration, or niche markets? Fox, more than any other network, could provide a representational bridge to the future. Neither blatantly homeboyish like its successors, nor as Wonder Breadish as the original three networks, the fourth network has now set its sights on an "organic" multiculturalism.

"There's *Friends,*" said Yvette Lee Bowser, "which is white characters finding out about love and life. And there's *Living Single,* which is black characters finding out about love and life. The only thing missing now is integrated shows." In fact, Bowser had hit on what seemed to be the next trend for mainstream networks. In the summer of 1998, both Fox and ABC announced plans to air *Captivity* and *The Hughleys* (co-executive produced by Chris Rock), respectively—two comedies about black couples moving into white suburban neighborhoods. "It's not about sticking a thermometer up the butt of networks," agreed David Mills, who has written for such critically acclaimed multiethnic dramas as *Picket Fences, ER, NYPD Blue,* and *Homicide.* The challenge of the future, says Mills, is to create characters like those played by Andre Brauer (*Homicide*) and Eriq LaSalle (*ER*): characters who "transcend" race. "The fact that Brauer plays a tortured, Jesuit-educated man, and that [*Homicide* producer] Tom Fontana used his own background to write a black character is to be congratulated," says Mills. "Such shows present our humanity without pimping blackness."

In the meantime, it would serve us well to remember that where integration fails, African Americans will always find ways to talk to one another, to dream and desire collectively. The Fox network of the early 1990s was one such place. Almost by accident, the fourth network nurtured dramatic episodes of *The Fresh Prince of Bel Air, The Sinbad Show,* and *South Central* that addressed intraracial classism and colorism; episodes of *Martin* and *Living Single* that looked at issues of black sexuality, gender, and romance; *Roc* that asked us to define a contemporary model of social responsibility and collective action; and *New York Undercover* that wrestled with shared yearnings among African Americans and Latinos.

Like a blast of fresh air after rain, African American productions of the early 1990s allowed us to inhale just a bit deeper, to reflect a fraction of a dramatic minute longer. Such shows helped us to know that our fears, desires, and memories are often collective, not individual. We may have been watching alone in our homes, but black shows of the 1990s were not unlike those conversations our grandparents used to have on front porches, in segregated cities, so far away from home.

Notes

Introduction

1. Many others have challenged the notion of "authenticity" and the totalizing assumptions upon which "belonging" is based. Jill Nelson's witty description of this struggle is one of my favorites: "For a few years in my early 20s, I stopped going to [Martha's] Vineyard in the summer, convinced that it was not an authentic Negro experience. That the beauty of gingerbread cottages, the red cliffs of Gay Head, the ocean right outside my doorstep, the Nelsons's own private, self-cleaning pool was not sufficiently down and dirty to qualify as a valid entry in the collective racial experience" (Fraser, 60).

2. In fact, Fox was not legally a network at all. In order to avoid the high costs of such a venture, owner Rupert Murdoch manipulated Federal Communications Commission requirements by offering just under fifteen hours of prime-time programming per week. Fox's parent company, the News Corporation, was a sprawling conglomerate that included the 20th Century Fox Film Corporation, Twentieth Television, and the Fox Broadcasting Corporation. The News Corporation remains today the world's largest media entity and the second largest publisher in the United States, with holdings in *TV Guide, Financial Times, The Economist,* HarperCollins, Viking, and Penguin (Bagdikian, 241). Having said this, I will follow the dictates of common usage here and refer to Fox as a "network."

3. See Nielsen 1987 and Alligood.

4. See David Atkin for a summary of NBC and black programming. By the early 1990s, ABC's lineup also included black-cast comedies such as *Family Matters, Hangin' with Mr. Cooper,* and *Sister, Sister.* However, these were not black productions in that they were not headed by majority-black production staffs.

5. Unless otherwise noted, all quotes are from interviews with the author.

6. Feinberg, 3.

7. Block, 275.

8. Harris, 39.

9. Gates 1987. For more on Claudia Mitchell-Kernan's definition of signifying see Kochman.

10. See John Tulloch and Manuel Alvarado, Norma Schulman, Tricia Rose. Schulman borrows Deleuze and Guattari's notion of a "minor discourse" to talk specifically about black sitcoms. I find her reading problematic, however, as it categorically labels *Roc, The Fresh Prince of Bel Air, South Central,* and *The Sinbad Show* "assimilationist" narratives. My overriding point in this book is that such shows reveal, more accurately, a desire for that which is both African and American.

11. Also see Alperstein, who describes "imaginary social relationships" between viewers and actors based on gossip and prior media exposure.

12. Also see Gray 1989.

13. As Fredric Jameson makes clear in his classic study *The Political Unconscious*: "[Art] constitutes a symbolic act, whereby real social contradictions, insurmountable in their own terms, find a purely formal resolution in the aesthetic realm. . . . From this perspective, ideology is not something which informs or invests symbolic production; rather the aesthetic act is . . . to be seen as an ideological act in its own right" (70).

14. From a phone conversation with Eric Hanks, owner of M. Hanks Art Gallery and brother to Camille Cosby. Further extratextual ties may be seen in Bill Cosby's bestselling children's book, *Money Troubles,* which contains illustrations by Varnette Honeywood.

15. This description of *The Bill Cosby Show* is J. Fred MacDonald's, 1990, 118.

16. I thank Reebee Garofolo for alerting me to this point.

17. This is largely Ella Taylor's definition of a dramedy, 154.

18. Reid, 5. In fact Reid went on to create and co-executive produce, together with Susan Fales, yet another dramedy in 1998 called *Linc's.* Debuting to rave reviews on Showtime, the series (directed by Debbie Allen) again addressed intraracial class issues as well as what Reid called "black homophobia." And yet having an executive producer credit does not always guarantee creative freedom, as Reid reminded me in 1994. "I had control on *Snoops,*" he noted. "I had a certain amount of shared control on *Frank's Place.* Anything you see my name on, I'm gonna exercise control. However, in doing so you can antagonize the system. You can cause yourself to be in contention with the structure of network television

that can create an atmosphere in which you don't get the proper enthusiasm for your project, especially if you're African American."

19. MacDonald 1990, 286.

20. A word on the ratings excuse: Warner Brothers (parent company of HBO/HIP) research confirms that *Roc*'s average ratings for 1991–92 were 13–14, about right for Fox. In 1993, the show was moved from Sunday to Thursday, and ratings predictably dropped. *Martin,* meanwhile, was placed in *Roc*'s former Sunday slot, where it garnered an average of 14. As these figures suggest, *Roc*'s ratings were less an indication of audience rejection than of network scheduling practices. In fact, black audiences preferred *Roc* (number 2) to *Martin* (number 4). The problem was that Fox was now interested in white audiences, which preferred *Martin.* See also Zook, "Dismantling *M.A.N.T.I.S.*," for a description of how one show was rewritten to reflect the network's shift from an Afrocentric aesthetic to one more suitable for white audiences.

Chapter 1

1. Both the opening credit sequence and Will Smith's sitcom persona borrow from the Fresh Prince music video "Parents Just Don't Understand."

2. Much of this autobiographical outline is taken from Carolyn Brown.

3. MacDonald, 249–50.

4. Friend.

5. See Sherwood's "Will Smith." It should be noted however, that in this article, Sherwood oddly describes *The Fresh Prince* as a show that emphasizes family over race. More accurately, I would say that the text explores whether or not the black "race" should continue to define itself as "family."

6. Ressner.

7. Hammer, 71.

8. Hersey.

9. Newman.

10. Sherwood, "A Real Life Prince."

11. Dent, 54.

12. Nielsen 1990.

13. The casting of Glenn Plummer as Top Dog is full of rich intertextual connotations. In feature films, *South Central,* and *Menace II Society,* Plummer plays convicted criminals and ex-gang members. In *South Central,* his character even argues that gangs (read here: fraternities) only offer the *illusion* of safety, whereas true loyalty is in blood relations.

14. A humorous tag scene following commercials provides relief, however, from this otherwise dramatic conclusion.

15. From NBC press notes.

16. Udovitch.

17. Rohter. And yet the struggle for authorship continued. In a rare episode written by Medina, Vivian Banks chastizes Will for flaunting Africa medallions, "Free Nelson Mandela" buttons, and *The Autobiography of Malcolm X,* as if these were proof of racial authority. "Baby, you can read that book," she tells him. "You can wear the T-shirts, you can put up the posters, and you can shout the slogans. But unless you know *all* the history behind it, you're trivializing the entire struggle."

18. Coker.

Chapter 2

1. Tom.

2. Tom. *Me and the Boys* (ABC) was a similarly themed show that debuted in 1995. In it, African American comic Steve Harvey—a real-life divorced father of twin daughters—also liked the idea of playing a responsible, single father. Although the show ranked fifteenth in total households, it was canceled at the end of its first season, ostensibly due to poor ratings. Steve Harvey, however, later returned with the highly similar *Steve Harvey Show,* which aired on the Warner Brothers network.

3. Tom.

4. Tom.

5. Dreifus.

6. From an interview with co-producer Calvin Brown Jr., who also belonged to a black fraternity and shared Farquhar's reservations.

7. Like the real-life practice of New Orleans social clubs which did in fact require members to be lighter than brown paper bags, this issue was also addressed on *Frank's Place,* where Creoles attempted to stave off discrimination charges by persuading Frank (Tim Reid) to join their group. On that show, Frank declined saying that he has no interest in being "the only black in a black club."

8. When I presented this to Sinbad, he couldn't recall whether or not the laughter was "natural" or "canned" in this instance. He did agree, however, that it was an unusual place for laughter.

9. I borrow this term from Benedict Anderson.

10. The show was canceled after its first season. As we shall see time and again in this book, network arguments that audiences aren't interest-

ed in "issues" is debatable: *The Sinbad Show* ranked eighth among black viewers at the time of its cancellation. The problem was that Fox was now interested in white viewers.

Chapter 3

1. In something of a non sequitur, Tortorici then added: "and I don't think the two are mutually exclusive." See Du Brow 1994.

2. See Shales and DuBrow 1994, respectively.

3. Nicole's materialism is later reincarnated on NBC's *In the House* (a Winifred Hervey/Quincy Jones production), where the same actress, Maia Campbell, again plays a snooty, upper-income teen. Women are not always presented monolithically on *South Central,* though. When Joan's best friend asks why she doesn't just marry Dr. McHenry ("Isn't $100,000 a year good enough?"), Joan protests that he simply "doesn't turn her on."

4. Another ironic case of intertextuality: In the feature film *House Party 3* Angela Means again plays a rich girl engaged to marry a man her family doesn't approve of, while her fiancé's uncle is played by Bernie Mac!

5. Another possibility is that white executives "got it" but didn't like it. Some particularly bold dialogue has a customer noting that white NBA owners don't like to see black men with "their" women. "Man, what you talking about?" responds Bernie. "Every [white] brother in sports got a white woman. . . . That's how the white man get his money back."

6. There are also similarities between the two shows that viewers may not be aware of. Aesthetically, for example, both utilize the same Ujamaa set. Although it was revamped as a black-owned café for *Moesha,* residual signs of Africanesqueness remain. Moreover, both series were committed to hiring a majority of African American writers and staff members. In 1998, *Moesha*'s staff was listed by the Writer's Guild of America as having the highest percentage of black writers on any show—with a total of eight African Americans and one Latina.

Chapter 4

1. I borrow here from Ru Paul's definition of the term as "a comical style of drag where you have hair on your legs and chest."

2. *Martin* supporters might point out that the tag scene of this episode has Pam having the same dream—smiling as she kills Martin. I would say that this bit serves only to assuage the episode's misogyny, not to refute it.

3. Again *Martin* supporters might point to the conclusion as evidence of "progressive" thinking, since Martin eventually reassures Gina that he loves her the way she is. But such a contorted narrative could also be read as the text's contradictory response to black female subjectivity.

4. Sheneneh also bears a striking resemblance to Jamie Foxx's drag characterization of Ugly Wanda, formerly seen on *In Living Color.* When pregnant Wanda is ready to give birth, she takes herself to the hospital, where she's treated like an animal. ("What is it?" shout the medical staff upon seeing her.) And in a highly tasteless labor scene, a black doll actually *shoots forth* from Wanda's open legs, sails across the room, and attacks a doctor. In a remarkably similar episode of *Martin,* an acquaintance of Pam's gives birth on Martin's couch, where a black doll is again torpedoed from her open legs before attacking a terrified Martin.

5. Sherwood, "Scene Stealers."

6. My research included speaking to former colleagues of both Lawrence and Campbell. One source who worked on *Boomerang,* a 1992 film in which Lawrence had a featured role, confirms that the actor was unpredictable and "manic" even then. "One minute he was the sweetest, nicest guy, almost soft-spoken," said the source. "And the next, he was ranting and raving because his trailer wasn't as big as David Alan Grier's." A crew member who worked on *Martin* agreed that working with Lawrence was like "walking on eggshells . . . sometimes he'd be the nicest, most polite young man. But then he'd flip a switch. He'd become a tyrant, violent and mean." I'm indebted here to John Griffiths, who provided me with research assistance. Both Campbell and Lawrence declined repeated requests for interviews.

7. Former *Martin* staff writer Darice Rollins later admitted: "If it made us laugh, we put on blinders to some issues. [But] some of the beady-bee jokes *did* get to be too much. . . . And the big butt jokes. Pam was always getting slammed."

8. *Jet,* April 15, 1996.

9. Ibid.

10. Zook, "Still Waiting."

11. Examples of such aesthetic and political allegiances included Lawrence wearing a "Free Mike Tyson" T-shirt in one episode, and a Spike Lee commercial that was frequently aired during *Martin.* In the latter, an ad for AT&T, Lee sits in the bedroom of an African American teen awaiting his girlfriend's call. Eventually the director intimates that the girlfriend (a cheerleader) may not have called because she likes one of the basketball players. With this, the boy begins to sweat profusely. As endearing as this commercial is, it also naturalizes male desire for possession and own-

ership of the female body, performing an unmistakable function within the "flow" of Martin.

Chapter 5

1. During the 1996–97 season, Khadijah is so bedazzled by an $8,000 diamond engagement ring that she blindly accepts a marriage proposal, only to back out later. Meanwhile, Regine kicks herself for having rejected a wealthy entrepreneur before learning of his assets.

2. Collier, February 1996.

3. This is Alice Walker's term, who offers this definition: "Womanist is to feminist as purple to lavender." See Walker 1983.

4. Autobiographical content is often subtle, but definitely present in Bowser's productions. For example, the writer-producer is biracial. In *Living Single,* Synclaire is also depicted as the biracial daughter of a white mother and a black father, as is Karyn Parsons's character, Margot, in *Lush Life,* a pilot also created by Bowser.

5. Collier 1996.

6. Lane.

7. Gregory.

8. Rose. Permission to reprint these and other Latifah lyrics was denied by the rapper, due to a possible "conflict of interest" with her own forthcoming book.

9. Lynell George.

10. I'm enormously indebted to Elliott Butler-Evans here, whose *Race, Gender and Desire* was the first to highlight this tension in the literary works of Toni Cade Bambara, Alice Walker, and Toni Morrison.

11. Alan Carter.

12. Danyel Smith.

13. Linden.

14. Gregory, 60.

15. Collier 1993, 116.

Chapter 6

1. If black television is in fact a collective autobiographical narrative about our psychic and material integration, Lathan's presence throughout this book (*Roc, The Sinbad Show, South Central, Pearl's Place to Play, Moesha,* and *Martin*) is certainly fitting. In 1968 the director got

his break on *Black Journal,* the first national news program to be produced and directed by African Americans.

2. In fact, Sinbad credited Charles Dutton with influencing his approach to *The Sinbad Show.* During a guest appearance on *Roc,* in 1993, the comedian recalled watching Dutton closely. "He would read the script and all of a sudden it would get quiet," noted Sinbad. He'd look up and say, 'Everybody just go to lunch. I ain't doing this.' Somebody would say [in a nasal voice], 'Oh, come on, it's just comedy.' And he'd say, 'Not with us, it's not.' "

3. Cornel West calls this the "conservative behavioral" approach to crime, whereby individuals rather than institutions are seen as responsible for the mess we're in. This is in opposition to the "liberal structuralist" viewpoint, which holds government, corporate, educational, and social structures accountable as well. See Cornell West 1993, Gray 1989, Hamamoto, and Lewis Freeman on the problem of individual rather than structural narratives in television. Interestingly, a similar presentational speech appears at the conclusion of the *Menace II Society* home video. Sponsored by the Institute for Black Parenting, this "special message from Charles Dutton" warns that "turning away from violence and rebuilding the community is *your* responsibility, not someone else's."

4. Ironically, this episode begins with a promotional spot for *The Simpsons* in which Homer Simpson also "declares war on crime." In the promo, cartoon community members are seen armed with rifles against graffiti "taggers" as Homer Simpson vows to "whip the neighborhood into shape." Within this same promotional sequence a clip for *America's Most Wanted* spins by with the image of a bloodied black female body and the mug shot of a black man. Needless to say these clips are troubling in that they work with *Roc*'s narrative to foreground notions of criminality as inherently "black."

5. Davis 1992. Fredric Jameson's Marxist analysis is fitting here. He writes: "To propose religious and ritual practices as a symbolic way of affirming social unity in a society which is objectively class divided, is clearly an ideological operation and an attempt to conjure such divisions away by an appeal to some higher (and imaginary) principle of collective and social unity. See *The Political Unconscious,* 292.

6. Interestingly, this same image appears in artwork hung in Kyle and Overton's apartment on *Living Single.*

7. In addition to these, a subsequent episode has Andre Thompson visiting Terence's murderer in prison. The scene was certainly an example of collective autobiographical dialogue, given that one in three young black men is in some way involved with the criminal justice system, as was Dutton himself prior to becoming an actor.

Chapter 7

1. Not only was it number one, *Undercover* had the highest concentration of black viewers—54 percent, of any show on air (Battaglio 1995). Unfortunately, Nielsen did not keep such figures for Latino viewers at the time. As Elena Soto, president of Katz Hispanic Media notes, advertisers have begun only recently to court Latinos, realizing that they spend disproportionate sums of money on goods and services such as children's clothing, beef, cereal, telephone calls, and cleaning supplies. See Cooper.

2. In the third season, the balance shifted back somewhat with the addition of African American writers Gar Anthony Haywood and Denetria Harris, who brought the ratio of nonwhite writers to five on a staff of seven.

3. Gaines.

4. This episode resonates autobiographically with Yoba's own experience. The actor has been involved with New York youth organizations since the age of seventeen, following a gunshot wound to the neck. It is also fascinating to note that the story line is virtually identical to that of the original *M.A.N.T.I.S.* movie (Fox) in which a man appearing to be a black nationalist hero is actually the dirtiest of crooks.

5. A particularly fitting question in the context of a promotional clip for Fox news, also aired during this episode. In this clip, a report on "kids who kill" shows a handcuffed youth wearing baggy "cholo" jeans and facing a judge alongside an American flag.

6. Davidson.

7. It could be said that DeLorenzo's firing had nothing to do with race, that he had simply picked an inopportune moment to ask for a pay raise. And yet Yoba, who also asked for a raise and better working conditions, was returned to the series.

8. Interestingly, Wolf had tried earlier to spin off *Undercover* with a similarly themed series called *Feds.* This one-hour cop show was everything *Undercover* had been, minus the African American and Latino leads. Wolf finally succeeded, not with this show but with *Players*, another mutation of *Undercover* starring Ice-T (and several white cast members) and co-created by Reggie Bythewood.

Conclusion

1. Hettrick.

2. Holsendolph 1995.

3. President Clinton, meanwhile, expressed regret that he had not been better able to "deal with the Murdoch situation" as he might have done had he possessed the power of line-item veto.

4. Stern. Murdoch has also avoided paying his fair share of taxes. Whereas most large corporations—be they American, British, or Australian—pay between 20 percent and 40 percent of their taxable income, Murdoch's global empire paid less than 7 percent in 1995, by using a system of "intra-company loans." Cowe.

5. Even a powerhouse such as Quincy Jones—who shares control of Quincy Jones–David Salzman Entertainment (QDE), Qwest Broadcasting, and *Vibe* Magazine with Time Warner, Warner, and Time Ventures, respectively—does not participate in a single venture in which black ownership exceeds 50 percent. Another case in point is that of Black Entertainment Television (BET). Although commonly perceived as black-owned, due to its highly visible African American shareholder Robert Johnson, the subscription service was founded with Johnson's borrowed $15,000 and $500,000 invested by John Malone's TCI. See Trescott, *Emerge* 1995: 66.

6. As former president of network distribution for Fox Broadcasting, Preston Padden noted, "The NFL . . . marked the point in time when Rupert Murdoch decided he was not content to be the fourth network. He wanted to be number one." See Don West, 18.

7. Cerone, January 2, 1995.

8. Tobenkin.

9. 1994 NBC dramas such as *The Cosby Mysteries* and *Sweet Justice* were equally disappointing. Although they starred Bill Cosby and Cicely Tyson as "positive" professionals (a detective and an attorney, respectively), these shows were essentially white productions that situated African American viewers in uncomplicated, non-race specific ways.

10. Other possibilities for black authorship and collective autobiography might resemble ventures such as the African Heritage Network, a minority syndicator owned by Frank Mercado-Valdes and Baruch Entertainment. A similar enterprise was the now-defunct World African Network headed by Phyllis and Eugene Jackson, with backing from Clarence Avant, Percy Sutton, and Sidney Small. Although this premium channel "dedicated to the cultural uplift of African descendants" never materialized, it was a fascinating study in self-representation. Its founders planned to use what they called an "Africanity index" to rate the "cultural correctness" of its programming.

11. Jacobs, 15.

References

Works Consulted

African Americans: Voices of Triumph. By the editors of Time–Life Books. Forward by Henry Louis Gates, Jr. Alexandria, VA: Time–Life, 1993.

Ajaye, Franklin. "You Can't Always Do What You Want to Do: Writing for 'In Living Color,'" *Emerge,* October 1990: 90–91.

Allen, Robert C., ed. *Channels of Discourse.* Chapel Hill: University of North Carolina Press, 1987.

Alligood, Doug. "Monday Memo." *Broadcasting and Cable,* April 26, 1993: 74.

Alperstein, Neil M. "Imaginary Social Relationships with Celebrities Appearing in Television Commercials." *Journal of Broadcasting and Electronic Media* 35, no. 1 (Winter 1991): 43–58.

Alterman, Eric. "Prizing Murdoch." *The Nation,* June 23, 1997: 6–7.

Alvarado, Manuel, and John Thompson, eds. *The Media Reader.* London: British Film Institute, 1990.

Anderson, Benedict. *Imagined Communities: Reflections on the Origin and Spread of Nationalism.* London: Verso, 1983.

Andrews, William. "Toward A Poetics of Afro–American Autobiography." In *Afro-American Literary Study in the 1990s,* edited by Houston A. Baker Jr. and Patricia Redmond. Chicago: University of Chicago Press, 1989.

———. "Biography and Autobiography, and Afro-American Culture" *Yale Review* 73, no. 1 (October 1983): 1–16.

Ang, Ien. *Desperately Seeking the Audience.* London and New York: Routledge, 1991.

Asante, Molefi Kete. *Afrocentricity: The Theory of Social Change.* New York: Amulefi Publishing Company, 1980.

Atkin, David. "An Analysis of Television Series with Minority-Lead Characters." *Critical Studies in Mass Communication* 9, no. 4 (December 1992): 337–49.

REFERENCES

Aubry, Erin and Greg Braxton. "South Central Tunes Itself In." *Los Angeles Times,* April 7, 1994: B1.

Auletta, Ken. *Three Blind Mice: How the TV Networks Lost Their Way.* New York: Vintage Books, 1991.

———. "The Pirate." *The New Yorker,* November 13, 1995: 80–93.

Auter, P. J., and D. M. Davis. "When Characters Speak Directly to Viewers: Breaking the Fourth Wall in Television." *Journalism Quarterly* 68, nos. 1–2 (Spring/Summer 1991): 165–71.

Bagdikian, Ben. *The Media Monopoly.* Boston: Beacon Press, 1983.

Baker, C. Edwin. "Mergerphobia." *The Nation,* November 8, 1993: 520–21.

Baker, Houston, Jr. *Blues, Ideology, and Afro-American Literature: A Vernacular Theory.* Chicago, University of Chicago Press, 1984.

———. *Black Studies, Rap, and the Academy.* Chicago: University of Chicago Press, 1993.

Baker, Houston, Jr., and Patricia Redmond, eds. *Afro-American Literary Study in the 1990s.* Chicago: University of Chicago Press, 1989.

Balio, Tino. "Introduction to Part II." In *Hollywood in the Age of Television,* edited by Tino Balio. Boston: Unwin Hyman, 1990.

Bambara, Toni Cade. *The Seabirds Are Still Alive.* New York: Vintage, 1974.

———. *The Salt Eaters.* New York: Vintage, 1980.

———. "What It Is I Think I'm Doing Anyhow." *The Writer on Her Work.* Janet Sternburg, ed. New York: W.W. Norton and Co., 1980.

———. *Gorilla, My Love.* New York: Vintage, 1981 [1960].

———, ed. *The Black Woman.* New York: Mentor Books, 1970.

Bambara, Toni Cade. *Deep Sightings and Resue Missions: Fiction, Essays and Conversations.* New York: Pantheon Books, 1996.

Barnes, Marian E., and Linda Goss, eds. *Talk that Talk: An Anthology of African-American Storytelling.* New York: Simon and Schuster, 1989.

Barnouw, Erik. *Tube Of Plenty: The Evolution of American Television.* 2nd ed. New York: Oxford University Press, 1990.

Bates, Karen Grigsby. "Where's the Color on Primetime TV?" *Los Angeles Times,* September 19, 1997: B9.

Battaglio, Stephen. "Fox Net Keeps Its Edge with Black Households," *Hollywood Reporter,* March 21, 1995: 4.

———. "Black Viewers Warm up to Casting on WB, UPN." *Hollywood Reporter,* March 7, 1996: 6.

———. "Young Nets in the Hood: UPN, WB Wooing Blacks." *Hollywood Reporter,* May 17–19, 1996: 1.

Bennett, Tony, ed. *Popular Fiction: Technology, Ideology, Production, Reading.* New York: Routledge, 1990.

Berkman, Meredith. "Does Martin Have Legs?" *Entertainment Weekly,* February 4, 1994: 18–21.

Blau, Andrew. "Soapbox Among the Soaps." *Index on Censorship* 22, no. 2 (February 1993): 5.

Block, Alex Ben. *Outfoxed: Marvin Davis, Barry Diller, Rupert Murdoch, Joan Rivers, and the Inside Story of America's Fourth Television Network.* New York: St. Martin's, 1990.

Bobo, Jacqueline. "Black Women in Fiction and Nonfiction: Images of Power and Powerlessness." *Wide Angle,* 13, (nos. 3–4) 1991: 72–81.

Bogart, Leo. "Shaping a New Media Policy." *The Nation,* July 12, 1993: 57–60.

Bogle, Donald. *Toms, Coons, Mulattoes, Mammies and Bucks: An Interpretative History of Blacks in American Films.* New York: Continuum, 1989.

Boliek, Brooks. "FCC Revisiting Fox Ownership." *Hollywood Reporter,* June 3–5, 1994: 1.

———. "President Signs off on End to Minority Tax Break." *Hollywood Reporter,* April 12, 1995: 4, 22.

Boskin, Joseph. *Sambo: The Rise and Demise of an American Jester.* New York: Oxford University Press, 1986.

Bracey, John, August Meier, Elliott Rudwick, et al., eds. *Black Nationalism in America.* New York: Bobbs–Merrill, 1970.

———. "Hip-Hop TV's Leading Edge." *Los Angeles Times,* Calendar section, November 4, 1990: 9.

———. "To Him, Rap's No Laughing Matter." *Los Angeles Times,* Calendar section, July 14, 1991: 4.

———. "Where More Isn't Much Better." *Los Angeles Times,* Calendar section, October 4, 1992: 3.

Braxton, Greg. "Has NBC Given Up on Black Shows?" *Los Angeles Times,* June 16, 1993: F1.

———. "Has Black Comedy Been Beaten Blue?" *Los Angeles Times,* Calendar section, February 20, 1994: 5.

———. "Jackson Calls TV Racist, Urges Action." *Los Angeles Times,* July 26, 1994: B1.

———. "Campbell Returns to *Martin.*" *Los Angeles Times,* Calendar section, March 21, 1997: F1.

Brennan, Steve. "FBC Turns 'Page' for 'Wanted.'" *Hollywood Reporter,* January 14–16, 1994: 12.

Brooks, Tim, and Earle Marsh. *The Complete Director to Prime Time Network and Cable TV Shows, 1946–present.* 6th ed. New York: Ballantine Books, 1995.

Brown, Carolyn M. "The Master of Trades." *Black Enterprise,* June 1996: 244–54.

Brown, Elaine. *A Taste of Power: A Black Woman's Story.* New York: Pantheon Books, 1992.

Brown, Les. *Encyclopedia of Television.* 3rd Edition. Detroit: Gale Research, 1992.

Brown, Malaika. "Sisterhood Televised." *American Visions,* April/May 1995: 42–3.

Brown, Rich. "BET Plans à la Carte Channel." *Broadcasting and Cable,* September 13, 1993: 24.

———. *Broadcasting and Cable.* "More Choices for Cable Subscribers." October 4, 1993: 32.

Brunsdon, Charlotte. "Text and Audience." In *Remote Control: Television, Audiences, and Cultural Power,* edited by Ellen Seiter, et al. London: Routledge, 1989.

Burns, Gary, and Robert Thompson. *Television Studies: Textual Analysis.* New York: Praeger, 1989.

Butler-Evans, Elliott. *Race, Gender and Desire: Narrative Strategies in the Fiction of Toni Cade Bambara, Toni Morrison, and Alice Walker.* Philadelphia: Temple University Press, 1989.

Carby, Hazel. *Reconstructing Womanhood: The Emergence of the Afro-American Woman Novelist.* New York: Oxford University Press, 1987.

Carey, James W. *Communication as Culture: Essays on Media and Society.* Boston: Unwin Hyman, 1989.

Carlisle, Rodney. *The Roots of Black Nationalism.* New York: Kennikat Press, 1975.

Carnevale, Mary Lu. "Control of Fox TV Sparks Controversy on Capitol Hill and Calls for Hearing." *Wall Street Journal,* June 13, 1994: B8.

Carter, Alan. "Single Minded." *Entertainment Weekly,* May 13, 1994: 31–33.

Carter, Bill. "Nervous TV Networks Are Trying the Untried." *New York Times,* September 6, 1990: C15, C18.

———. "Upstart Networks Court Blacks." *New York Times,* October 7, 1996: B1.

Cerone, Daniel Howard. "A More Grown-Up Look for Fox." *Los Angeles Times,* July 4, 1995: F1–F16.

———. "New Year Brings Two New Networks." *Los Angeles Times,* January 2, 1995: F1.

Cliff, Michelle. *Claiming An Identity They Taught Me to Despise.* Watertown, Mass.: Persephone Press, 1980.

———. *Abeng: A Novel.* New York: Crossing Press, 1984.

———. *The Land of Look Behind: Prose and Poetry.* New York: Firebrand, 1985.

———. *No Telephone to Heaven.* New York: Vintage, 1987.

———. *Bodies of Water.* New York: Dutton, 1990.

———. *Free Enterprise.* New York: Dutton-NAL-Penguin, 1993.

Coe, Steve. "Bickley/Warren: ABC's Powerful TGIF team." *Broadcasting and Cable,* October 17, 1994: 30.

Coker, Cheo Hodari. "Good Night, 'Prince.'" *Los Angeles Times,* Calendar section, May 20, 1996: F1, F8.

Collier, Aldore D. "Queen Latifah Reigns On and Off TV." *Ebony,* December 1993: 116–22.

———. "Behind the Scenes of *Living Single.*" *Ebony,* February 1996: 26–34.

Collins, Glenn. "Now Rap Is Bum-Rushing the Mainstream." *New York Times,* August 29, 1988.

Cooper, Jim. "Advertisers Rush Into Growing Market." *Broadcasting and Cable.* November 15, 1993: 46.

Cosby, Bill. *Fatherhood.* Garden City, N.Y.: Doubleday, 1986.

———. *Money Troubles.* Illustrated by Varnette P. Honeywood. New York: Scholastic Inc., 1998.

Cowe, Roger, and Lisa Buckingham. "Murdoch and His Small Tax Secret." *The Guardian Weekly,* July 28, 1996: 14.

Cruse, Harold W. *The Crisis of the Negro Intellectual.* New York: Morrow, 1967.

Curtin, Michael. "Beyond the Vast Wasteland: The Policy Discourse of Global Television and the Politics of American Empire." *Journal of Broadcasting and Electronic Media* 37, no. 2. (Spring 1993): 127–45.

Daniels, Therese, and Jane Gerson. *The Colour Black: Black Images in British Television.* London: British Film Institute, 1989.

Dates, Jannette L., and William Barlow. *Split Image: African Americans in the Mass Media.* Washington, D.C.: Howard University Press, 1990.

Davidson, Mary Gray. "Puerto Rico, Island in Limbo." *Courier,* No. 16, Summer 1994: 12.

Davies, Jonathan. "WB Defends New Black Shows." *Hollywood Reporter,* July 9, 1996: 6.

Davis, Angela. *Women, Culture and Politics.* New York: Vintage Books, 1990.

———. "Black Nationalism: The Sixties and the Nineties." In *Black Popular Culture: A Project by Michele Wallace,* edited by Gina Dent. Seattle: Bay Press, 1992.

de Lauretis, Teresa. *Alice Doesn't: Feminism, Semiotics, Cinema.* Bloomington: Indiana University Press, 1984.

———. *Technologies of Gender: Essays on Theory, Film, and Fiction.* Bloomington: Indiana University Press, 1987.

———, ed. *Feminist Studies/Critical Studies.* Bloomington: Indiana University Press, 1986.

Deleuze, Gilles, and Felix Guattari. "What Is a Minor Literature?" in *Kafka: Toward a Minor Literature,* translated by Dana Polan. Minneapolis: University of Minnesota Press, 1986.

Dempsey, John. "Pricey Spots for Bel Air Rapper." *Variety*, September 10, 1990.

Dent, Gina, ed. *Black Popular Culture: A Project by Michele Wallace.* Seattle: Bay Press, 1992.

Diawara, Manthia, ed. *Black American Cinema.* New York: Routledge, 1993.

Dibbell, Julian. "It's The End of T.V. as We Know It." *Village Voice,* December 22, 1992: 55–60.

Di Leo, Michael. "Unbelievable Hype." *Mother Jones,* February–March 1989: 10.

Di Prima, Dominique. "Beat the Rap." *Mother Jones,* September–October 1990: 32.

Downing, John. "The Political Economy of U.S. Television." *Monthly Review,* May 1990: 30–41.

Draper, Theodore. *The Rediscovery of Black Nationalism.* London: Secker and Warburg, 1969.

———. "The Fantasy of Black Nationalism." *Commentary* 48, no. 3 (September 1969): 27–54.

Dreifus, Claudia. "Original Sinbad." *TV Guide,* November 27, 1993: 34.

Du Brow, Rick. "South Central: The Right Time, the Right Stuff." *Los Angeles Times,* Calendar section, January 11, 1994: F1.

———. "The Reason *Boys* Didn't Make the Cut." *Los Angeles Times,* May 18, 1995: F1.

Dyson, Michael Eric. "Bill Cosby and the Politics of Race," *Z Magazine,* September 1989: 26–30.

———. *Reflecting Black: African-American Cultural Criticism.* Minneapolis: University of Minnesota Press, 1993.

———. *Making Malcolm: The Myth and Meaning of Malcolm X.* New York: Oxford University Press, 1995.

———. *Between God and Gangsta Rap: Bearing Witness to Black Culture.* New York: Oxford University Press, 1996.

———. *Race Rules: Navigating the Color Line.* Reading, Mass.: Addison-Wesley Pub., 1996.

Early, Gerald. *Tuxedo Junction: Essays on American Culture.* New York: Ecco Press, 1989.

———. "Their Malcolm, My Problem: On the Abuses of Afrocentrism and Black Anger," *Harper's,* December 1992: 62.

———, ed. *Lure and Loathing: Essays on Race, Identity, and the Ambivalance of Assimilation.* New York: Viking Penguin, 1993.

Eaton, Mick. "Television Situation Comedy." In *Popular Film and Television Comedy.* London: Routledge, 1990.

Ellis, John. *Visible Fictions: Cinema, Television, Video.* London: Routledge, 1982.

Ellis, Trey. "The New Black Aesthetic." *Callaloo* 12, no. 1 (Winter 1989): 233–43.

Enzensberger, Hans Magnus. *The Consciousness Industry: On Literature, Politics and the Media.* New York: Seabury, 1974.

Essien–Udom, E. U. *Black Nationalism: A Search for Identity in America.* New York: Dell Publishing, 1962.

Fabre, Genevieve, and Robert O'Meally, eds. *History and Memory in African American Culture.* New York: Oxford University Press, 1994.

Feinberg, Andrew. "TV Test-Drives New-Wave Comedy: Jerry, Carol and Keenen Go For Post-Sitcom Laughs." *TV Guide,* June 2, 1990: 3–6.

Ferguson, Russell, et al., eds. *Out There: Marginalization and Contemporary Cultures.* Cambridge: MIT Press, 1990.

Feuer, Jane. "Narrative Form in American Network Television." In *High Theory/Low Culture: Analyzing Popular Culture and Film,* edited by Colin MacCabe. Manchester: Manchester University Press, 1988.

———. "Genre Study and Television." In *Channels of Discourse,* edited by Robert C. Allen. Chapel Hill: University of North Carolina Press.

Fiske, John. *Television Culture: Popular Pleasures and Politics.* New York: Methuen, 1987.

———. *Reading Television.* New York: Routledge, 1989.

———. *Understanding Popular Culture.* Boston: Unwin Hyman, 1989.

———. *Media Matters: Everyday Culture and Political Change.* Minneapolis: University of Minnesota Press, 1994.

Fluck, Winfried. "Popular Culture as a Mode of Socialization: A Theory about the Social Functions of Popular Cultural Forms," *Journal of Popular Culture* 21. no. 3 (Winter 1987): 31–46.

———. "Fiction and Fictionality in Popular Culture: Some Observations on the Aesthetics of Popular Culture." *Journal of Popular Culture* 21, no. 4 (Spring 1988): 49–62.

Foster, Hal. *Recodings: Art, Spectacle, and Cultural Politics.* Port Townsend, Wash.: Bay, 1985.

Fraser, C. Gerald. "An 'Authentic' Experience." *Emerge,* July/August 1993: 60–61.

Frazier, E. Franklin. *Black Bourgeoisie: The Rise of a New Middle Class.* New York: Free Press, 1957.

Freeman, Lewis. "Social Mobility in Television Comedies." *Critical Studies in Mass Communication* 9, no. 4 (1992): 400–6.

Freeman, Mike. "Ratings Block Minority Syndicators." *Broadcasting and Cable,* September 27, 1993: 30–31.

Freud, Sigmund. *On Dreams,* edited and translated by James Strachey. New York: W. W. Norton and Company, 1952.

———. *Jokes and Their Relation to the Unconscious,* edited and translated by James Strachey. New York: W. W. Norton and Co., 1960.

Friend, Tad. "Sitcoms, Seriously." *Esquire,* March 1993: 112–25.

Frith, Simon. "Art Ideology and Pop Practice." In *Marxism and the Interpretation of Culture,* edited by Lawrence Grossberg and Cary Nelson. Urbana: University of Illinois Press, 1988.

Gabler, Neal. "Does Murdoch Mean the End of Romance in Media?" *Los Angeles Times,* June 5, 1994: 172.

Gaines, Steven. "Black Writer Blues." *Buzz,* October 1995: 39–42.

Garafolo, Reebee, ed. *Rockin' the Boat: Mass Music and Mass Movements.* Boston: South End Press, 1992.

Gates, Henry Louis, Jr. *Figures in Black: Words, Signs, and the "Racial" Self.* New York: Oxford University Press, 1987.

———. *The Signifying Monkey: A Theory of Afro-American Literary Criticism.* Oxford: Oxford University Press, 1988.

———, ed. *Race, Writing and Difference.* Chicago: University of Chicago Press, 1988.

———. "TV's Black World Turns—But Stays Unreal." *New York Times,* November 12, 1989, Arts and Leisure section: C1.

———. *Loose Canons: Notes On the Culture Wars.* New York: Oxford University Press, 1992.

Gay, Geneva, and Willie L. Baber, eds. *Expressively Black: The Cultural Basis of Ethnic Identity.* New York: Praeger, 1987.

Gaye, Vern. "TV Networks 'Colorize' More Programs." *Emerge,* September 1993: 51–2.

Gayle, Addison, Jr. *The Black Aesthetic.* New York: Doubleday, 1971.

George, Lynell. "This One's for the Ladies." In *No Crystal Stair: African Americans in the City of Angels.* London and New York: Verso, 1992.

George, Nelson. *The Death of Rhythm and Blues.* New York: Dutton, 1988.

———. *Buppies, B-Boys, Baps and Bohos: Notes on Post-Soul Black Culture.* New York: HarperCollins, 1992.

———, ed. *Stop the Violence: Overcoming Self-Destruction: Rap Speaks Out.* New York: National Urban League, 1990.

Gilroy, Paul. *There Ain't No Black in the Union Jack: The Cultural Politics of Race and Nation.* London: Hutchinson, 1987.

———. "It's a Family Affair." In *Black Popular Culture: A Project by Michele Wallace,* edited by Gina Dent. Seattle: Bay Press, 1992.

———. *The Black Atlantic: Modernity and Couble Consciousness.* Cambridge: Harvard University Press, 1993.

Gitlin, Todd. *The Whole World Is Watching: Mass Media in the Making and Unmaking of the New Left.* Berkeley: University of California Press, 1980.

———. *Inside Prime Time.* New York: Pantheon Books, 1983.

———. *Watching Television.* New York: Pantheon, 1986.

Goldberg, Robert. "Hip-Hop Cops." *TV Guide,* October 15, 1994: 28–31.

Gray, Herman. "Television and the New Black Man: Black Male Images in Prime Time Situation Comedy," *Media, Culture and Society* 8, 1986: 223–43.

———. "Television, Black Americans, and the American Dream." *Critical Studies in Mass Communication* 6, no. 4, December 1989: 376–86.

———. "The Endless Slide of Difference: Critical Television Studies, Television, and the Question of Race." *Critical Studies in Mass Communication.* Vol. 10, No. 2. June 1993: 190–197.

———. "African-American Political Desire and the Seductions of Contemporary Cultural Politics." *Cultural Studies.* Vol. 7, No. 3. October 1993: 363–73.

———. *Watching Race: Television and the Struggle for "Blackness."* Minneapolis: University of Minnesota Press, 1995.

Gregory, Deborah. "Rapping Back." *Essence,* August 1991: 57–60.

Grossberg, Lawrence, and Cary Nelson, eds. *Marxism and the Interpretation of Culture.* Urbana: University of Illinois Press, 1988.

Grover, Ronald. "How Fox Outfoxed Itself." *Business Week.* December 20, 1993: 48.

Guerrero, Ed. *Framing Blackness: The African American Image in Film.* Philadelphia: Temple University Press, 1993.

Gunther, Marc. "Black Producers Add a Fresh Nuance." *New York Times,* August 26, 1990, section 2.

Hager, Steven. *Hip Hop: The Illustrated History of Break Dancing, Rap Music and Graffiti.* New York: St. Martin's Press, 1984.

Hall, Stuart. "The Rediscovery of Ideology: Return of the Repressed in Media Studies." In *Culture, Society and Media,* edited by M. Gurevitch, et al. London: Methuen, 1982.

———. "Minimal Selves" and "New Ethnicities." In *ICA Documents,* edited by Lisa Appignanesi. London: Institute of Contemporary Arts, 1987.

———. "What Is This Black in Black Popular Culture?" In *Black Popular Culture: A Project by Michele Wallace,* edited by Gina Dent. Seattle: Bay Press, 1992.

———. "Culture, Community, Nation." *Cultural Studies.* 7, no. 3 (October 1993): 349–63.

———. "Notes on Deconstructing the Popular." In *People's History and Socialist Theory,* edited by Raphael Samuel. London: Routledge and Kegan Paul, 1981.

Hamamoto, Darrell Y. *Nervous Laughter: Television Situation Comedy and Liberal Democratic Ideology.* New York: Praeger, 1989.

Hammer, Joshua. "Must Blacks Be Buffoons?" *Newsweek*, October 26, 1992: 70–71.

Harris, Joanne. "Why Not Just Laugh? Making Fun of Ourselves on Television." *American Visions*, April–May 1993: 38–41.

Hartley, John. *Tele-ology: Studies in Television.* London: Routledge, 1992.

———. *Popular Reality: Journalism, Modernity, Popular Culture.* London: Arnold, 1996.

Hebdige, Dick. *Subculture: The Meaning of Style.* London: Methuen, 1979.

———. *Hiding in the Light: On Images and Things.* London: Comedia, 1988.

Henry, Charles P. *Culture and African American Politics.* Bloomington: Indiana University Press, 1990.

Hersey, Brook. *Glamour,* October 1990: 192.

Hettrick, Scott. "Jackson: Minority Media Off 15% on Tax Shift." *The Hollywood Reporter,* March 19, 1997: 6.

Hill, George, and Spencer Moon. *Blacks In Hollywood: Five Favorable Years in Film and Television, 1987–1991.* Los Angeles: Daystar, 1992.

Holsendolph, Ernest. "Eroding Support for Minority Broadcasters." *Emerge,* May 1995: 21–22.

———. "In Broadcasting, an Affirmative Action Success." *Emerge,* December/January 1996: 18.

hooks, bell. "Choosing the Margin as Space of Radical Openness." *Framework* 36 (1989): 15–23.

———. *Talking Back: Thinking Feminist, Thinking Black.* Boston: South End Press, 1989.

———. *Yearning: Race, Gender, and Cultural Politics.* Boston: South End Press, 1990.

———. *Black Looks: Race and Representation.* Boston: South End Press, 1992.

———. *Outlaw Culture: Resisting Representations.* New York: Routledge, 1994.

———. *Reel to Real: Race, Sex, and Class at the Movies.* New York: Routledge, 1996.

hooks, bell, and Cornel West. *Breaking Bread: Insurgent Black Intellectual Life.* Boston: South End Press, 1991.

Horowitz, Susan. "Sitcom Domesticus—A Species Endangered by Social Change." In *Television: The Critical View,* edited by Horace Newcomb. 4th ed. New York: Oxford University Press, 1987.

Hunter, Kristin. *God Bless the Child.* New York: Scribner, 1964.

———. *The Landlord.* New York: Scribner, 1966.

———. *The Soul Borthers and Sister Lou.* New York: Scribner, 1968.

———. *Guests in the Promised Land.* New York: Scribner, 1973.

———. *The Survivors.* New York: Scribner, 1975.

———. *The Lakestown Rebellion.* New York: Scribner, 1978.

———. *Lou in the Limelight.* New York: Scribner, 1981.

———. [Lattany] *Kinfolks.* New York: Ballantine Books, 1996.

Hurston, Zora Neale. *Mules and Men.* Introduction by Franz Boas. Philadelphia and London: J. B. Lippencott Company, 1935.

———. *Their Eyes Were Watching God.* New York: Negro Universities Press, 1937.

———. *Tell My Horse.* Philadelphia and New York: J. B. Lippencott Company, 1938.

———. *Dust Tracks on a Road.* New York: Arno Press, 1969 [1942].

———. *I Love Myself When I am Laughing . . . and Then Again When I am Looking Mean and Impressive: A Zora Neale Hurston Reader.* Edited by Alice Walker. Introduction by Mary Helen Washington. Old Westbury, N.Y.: Feminist Press, 1979.

———. *The Complete Stories.* Introduction by Henry Louis Gates, Jr. and Sieglinde Lemke. New York: Harper Collins, 1995.

Jackson, John Calloway. "A Rap Session With Queen Latifah." *Billboard,* November 27, 1993: 36, 52–54.

Jackson, Scoop. "To Live and Die in NY." *The Source,* September 1997: 91–96.

Jacobs, A. J. "Black to the Future: UPN and the WB's Focus on Black Shows Reignites Old Issues About TV's Color Barrier." *Entertainment Weekly,* June 14, 1996: 15–16.

Jameson, Fredric. *The Political Unconscious: Narrative as a Socially Symbolic Act.* Ithaca, N.Y.: Cornell University Press, 1981.

Jankowski, Gene F., and David C. Fuchs. *Television Today and Tomorrow: It Won't Be What You Think.* New York: Oxford University Press, 1995.

Jarvis, Jeff. "'*South Central*': The Couch Critic." *TV Guide,* May 21, 1994: 8.

Jet. "Wayans Surprised Whites Also Like *Living Color.*" November 12, 1990: 55.

Jet. "Martin Lawrence, Lynn Whitfield Star in New Movie 'A Thin Line Between Love and Hate.'" April 15, 1996: 32.

Jhally, Sut, and I. Angus, eds. *Cultural Politics in Contemporary America.* New York: Routledge, 1989.

Jhally, Sut, and Justin Lewis. *Enlightened Racism: The Cosby Show, Audiences, and the Myth of the American Dream.* Boulder: Westview Press, 1992.

Johnson, Charles. *Being and Race: Black Writing Since 1970.* Bloomington: Indiana University Press, 1988.

Kaplan, E. Ann. "Is the Gaze Male?" In *Powers of Desire: The Politics of Sexuality,* edited by Ann Snitow, Christine Stansell, and Sharon Thompson. New York: Monthly Review Press, 1983.

———. *Rocking Around the Clock: Music Television, Postmodernism and Consumer Culture.* New York: Methuen, 1987.

———, ed. *Regarding Television: Critical Approaches—An Anthology.* American Film Institute Monograph Series. Frederick, Md.: University Publications of America, 1983.

Kelley, Robin D. G. "Kickin' Reality, Kickin' Ballistics: The Cultural Politics of Gangsta Rap in Postindustrial Los Angeles." In *Droppin' Science: Critical Essays on Rap Music and Hip Hop Culture,* edited by Eric Perkins. Philadelphia: Temple University Press, 1994.

Kellner, Douglas. *Television and the Crisis of Democracy.* Boulder: Westview Press, 1990.

Kerr, Jane Alice. "Andy and Susan Borowitz." *New York Times,* September 9, 1990: H28.

Kinder, Marsha. "Music Video: TV, Ideology, and Dream." In *Television: The Critical View,* edited by Horace Newcomb. 4th ed. New York: Oxford University Press, 1987.

Kochman, Thomas. *Rappin' and Stylin' Out: Communication in Urban Black America.* Chicago: University of Illinois Press, 1972.

Kolbert, Elizabeth. "From 'Beulah' to 'Oprah': The Evolution of Black Images on TV." *New York Times,* January 15, 1993: B4.

Kronke, David. "Tip No. 1: Keep It Fresh." *Los Angeles Times,* Calendar section, March 17, 1996: 6.

Kruger, Barbara. *Remote Control: Power, Cultures, and the World of Appearances.* Cambridge, Mass.: MIT Press, 1993.

Lane, Christina. "The Liminal Iconography of Jodie Foster." *Journal of Popular Film and Television* 22, no. 4 (Winter 1995): 149–153.

Lanker, Brian. *I Dream a World: Portraits of Black Women Who Changed America,* edited by Barbara Summers. Foreword by Maya Angelou. New York: Tabori and Chang, 1989.

Layne, Barry. "Study Details Hispanic View of Television." *Hollywood Reporter,* September 17, 1993: 20.

Leland, John. "Rap and Race." *Newsweek,* June 29, 1992: 47–52.

Lemelle, Sidney J., and Robin D. G. Kelley, eds. *Imagining Home: Class, Culture and Nationalism in the African Diaspora.* London and New York: Verso, 1994.

Levine, Lawrence W. *Black Culture and Black Consciousness: Afro-American Folk Thought from Slavery to Freedom.* Oxford: Oxford University Press, 1977.

Levinson, Richard, and William Link. *Off Camera: Conversations with the Makers of Prime Time Television.* New York: New American Library, 1986.

Levy, Ellen. "The Packaging of America: Politics as Entertainment, Entertainment as Politics." *Dissent* 33 (1986): 441–46.

Linden, Amy. "Queen Latifah: From Here to Royalty." *The Source,* August 1998: 154–60.

Lorde, Audre. *The Black Unicorn: Poems.* New York: Norton, 1978.

———. *The Cancer Journals.* Second Edition. San Franciso: Spinsters, 1980.

———. *Zami: A New Spelling of My Name.* Trumansburg, N.Y.: Crossing Press, 1982.

———. *Sister Outsider: Essays and Speeches.* Trumansburg, N.Y.: Crossing Press, 1984.

———. *Our Dead Behind Us: Poems.* New York: Norton, 1986.

———. *A Burst of Light: Essays.* Ithaca, N.Y.: Firebrand Books, 1988.

———. *Need: A Chorale for Black Woman Voices.* Latham, N.Y.: Kitchen Table Press, 1990.

Lott, Eric. *Love and Theft: Blackface Minstrelsy and the American Working Class.* New York: Oxford University Press, 1993.

MacCabe, Colin, ed. *High Theory/Low Culture: Analysing Popular Television and Film.* Manchester: Manchester University Press, 1986.

MacDonald, J. Fred. *One Nation Under Television: The Rise and Decline of Network TV.* New York: Pantheon, 1990.

———. *Blacks and White TV: African-Americans in Television Since 1948.* 2nd edition. Chicago: Nelson-Hall, 1992.

MacKenzie, Robert. "The Fresh Prince of Bel Air." *TV Guide,* November 10, 1990: 48.

McAvoy, Kim. "Gore: Lack of Minority Ownership 'a Disgrace.'" *Broadcasting and Cable,* September 19, 1994: 6.

McCartney, John T. *Black Power Ideologies: An Essay in African-American Political Thought.* Philadelphia: Temple University Press, 1993.

McClellan, Steve. "Tribune, Minority Group on TV Station Qwest." *Broadcasting and Cable,* November 21, 1994: 8.

McNeil, Alex. *Total Television.* 4th Edition. New York: Penguin Books, 1996.

Marc, David. *Demographic Vistas: Television in American Culture.* Philadelphia: University of Pennsylvania Press, 1984.

———. *Comic Visions: Television Comedy and American Culture,* London: Unwin Hyman, 1989.

———. *Prime Time, Prime Movers: From "I Love Lucy" to "L.A. Law"—America's Greatest TV Shows and the People Who Created Them.* Boston: Little, Brown, 1992.

Mellencamp, Patricia. *The Logics of Television: Essays in Cultural Criticism:* Bloomington: Indiana University Press, 1990.

———. *High Anxiety: Catastrophe, Scandal, Age, and Comedy.* Bloomington: Indiana University Press, 1992.

Mercer, Kobena. "Black Hair/Style Politics." *New Formations* Vol. 3 (Winter 1987): 33–54.

———. *Welcome to the Jungle: New Positions in Black Cultural Studies.* New York: Routledge, 1994.

Merritt, Bishetta D. "Bill Cosby: TV Auteur?" *Journal of Popular Culture* 24, no. 4, (Spring 1991): 89–102.

Miller, Mark Crispin, ed. *Boxed In: The Culture of TV.* Evanston, Ill.: Northwestern University Press, 1988.

Milloy, Courtland. "Satire and Stereotype." *Washington Post,* October 7, 1990: B3.

Mills, David. "The Gangsta Rapper: Violent Hero or Negative Role Model?" *The Source,* December 1990: 31–40.

Modleski, Tania, ed. *Studies in Entertainment.* Bloomington: Indiana University Press, 1986.

Montgomery, Kathryn. *Target: Prime Time.* New York: Oxford University Press, 1989.

Nelson, Jill. *Volunteer Slavery: My Authentic Negro Experience.* New York, Penguin Books, 1993.

Nelson, Lars-Eric. "There's Money to Be Made on Big Bird." *Los Angeles Times,* January 31, 1995: B7.

Newcomb, Horace, ed. *Television: The Critical View.* 4th ed. New York: Oxford University Press, 1987.

Newcomb, Horace, and Robert Alley. *The Producer's Medium: Conversations with Creators of American TV.* New York: Oxford University Press, 1983.

Newman, Bruce. "A Cosmic Q Rating." *Los Angeles Times,* Calendar section, November 5, 1995: 4.

A. C. Nielsen Co. *Television Viewing Among Blacks: January–February 1987.* Northbrook, Ill.: A. C. Nielsen, 1987.

———. *Television Viewing Among Blacks: January–February 1988.* Northbrook, Ill.: A. C. Nielsen, 1988.

———. *Television Viewing Among Blacks: 1989–90.* Northbrook, Ill.: A. C. Nielsen, 1990.

———. *Black American Study: February 1995.* Northbrook, Ill.: A. C. Nielsen, 1995.

Noble, Gil. *Black Is the Color of My TV Tube.* New York: Lyle Stuart, 1990.

O'Connor, John J. "Veiling Black Rage in Broad Humor on TV." *New York Times,* January 31, 1991: C17.

———. "Beyond Slapstick to Show Perils Faced by Blacks." *New York Times,* April 5, 1994: C13, C18.

Omi, Michael. "*In Living Color*: Race and American Culture." In *Cultural Politics in Contemporary America,* edited by Ian Angus and Sut Jhally. London: Routledge, Chapman and Hall, 1989.

Owusu, Kwesi, ed. *Storms of the Heart: An Anthology of Black Arts and Culture.* London: Camden Press, 1988.

Pareles, Jon. "How Rap Moves to Television's Beat." *New York Times,* January 14, 1990: H1 (Section 2).

Parish, James Robert. *Today's Black Hollywood.* New York: Pinnacle Books, 1995.

Parker, Andrew, Mary Russo, et al., eds. *Nationalisms and Sexualities.* New York and London: Routledge, 1992.

Porter, Evette. "She Said/She Said." *Village Voice,* September 28, 1993: 50.

Press, Andrea. *Women Watching Television: Gender, Class, and Generation in the American Television Experience.* Philadelphia: University of Pennsylvania Press, 1991.

Pribam, E. Deidre, ed. *Female Spectators: Looking at Films and Television.* New York: Verso–New Left Books, 1988.

Rabinovitz, Lauren. "Television Criticism and American Studies." *American Quarterly* 43, no. 2 (June 1991): 258–370.

Rampersad, Arnold. "Biography and Autobiography, and AfroAmerican Culture." *Yale Review* 73, no. 1, (October 1983): 1–16.

Randolph, Laura B. "The Real-Life Fresh Prince of Bel Air: Television and Recording Tycoon Benny Medina Proves That Hollywood Life Can Be Stranger Than Hollywood Fiction." *Ebony,* April 1991: 30.

Rapping, Elayne. *Mediations: Forays Into the Culture and Gender Wars.* Boston: South End Press, 1994.

Reagon, Bernice Johnson. "My Black Mothers and Sisters, or On Beginning a Cultural Autobiography." *Feminist Studies* 8, no 1 (Spring 1982): 81–96.

Reid, Tim. "A Tale of Two Cultures: An Actor-Producer's Perspective During Black History Month." *Los Angeles Times,* TV Times section, February 20–26, 1994: 1, 5.

Ressner, Jeffrey. "Raps to Riches." *Rolling Stone,* September 20, 1990: 45.

Richmond, Ray. "TV Sitcoms: The Great Divide." *Variety,* April 13, 1998: 1.

Robb, David. "Doors Creaking Open to Latinos." *Hollywood Reporter,* December 30, 1993: 1.

Rohter, Larry. "*Fresh Prince of Bel Air* Puts Rap in Mainstream." *New York Times,* September 17, 1990: C17.

Rose, Tricia. *Black Noise: Rap Music and Black Culture in Contemporary America.* Middletown, Conn.: Wesleyan University Press; Hanover, N.H.: University Press of New England, 1994.

———. *Never Trust a Big Butt and a Smile.* New York: Oxford University Press, forthcoming.

Rosenberg, Howard. "A New Low on the Taste Meter." *Los Angeles Times,* December 15, 1993: F1, F8, F10.

———. "Fox Looks Inside 'South Central.'" *Los Angeles Times,* April 4, 1994: F1, F10.

———. "Don't Blame Fox TV for Trying to Reach Out." *Los Angeles Times,* October 17, 1994: F1.

Rosenthal, Herma M. "Rap Boogies in Upcoming Series, But Will Beat Go On and On?" *TV Guide,* August 4, 1990: 25.

Ross, Karen. *Black and White Media: Black Images in Popular Film and Television.* Cambridge, Mass.: Polity Press, 1996.

Rudolph, Ileane. "African Americans Viewing Habits on the Rise." *TV Guide,* March 26, 1994: 36.

Russo, Mary. "Female Grotesque: Carnival and Theory." In *Feminist Studies/Critical Studies,* edited by Teresa de Lauretis. Bloomington: Indiana University Press, 1986.

Schiller, Herbert. "Public Way or Private Road." *The Nation,* July 12, 1993: 64–66.

Schneider, Cynthia and Brian Wallis, eds. *Global Television.* Cambridge, Mass.: MIT Press, 1988.

Schone, Mark. "Rupert Don't Play That." *Village Voice,* October 10, 1995: 47.

Schulman, Norma Miriam. "Laughing Across the Color Line: In Living Color." *Journal of Popular Film and Television* 20, no. 1 (Spring 1992): 2–7.

———. "The House that Black Built: Television Stand-Up Comedy as Minor Discourse." *Journal of Popular Film and Television* 22, no. 3 (Fall 1994): 108–15.

Seiter, Ellen, et al., eds. *Remote Control: Television, Audiences and Cultural Power.* London: Routledge, 1989.

Seltzer, Richard, and Robert Smith. "Color Differences in the Afro-American Community and the Differences They Make." *Journal of Black Studies* 21, no. 3 (March 1991): 279–86.

Shak, Diane K. "Will Rupert Buy LA?" *Los Angeles Magazine,* December 1997: 108.

Shales, Tom. "Superior 'South Central.'" *Washington Post,* April 5, 1994: E1, E6.

Sherrill, Robert. "Citizen Murdoch: Buying His Way to a Media Empire." *The Nation,* May 29, 1995: 749–54.

Sherwood, Rick. "Dynamic Demo." *The Hollywood Reporter: Fresh Prince of Bel Air Salute,* September 16, 1994: S14.

———. "Hip Hop Hooray." *The Hollywood Reporter: Fresh Prince of Bel Air Salute,* September 16, 1994: S3.

———. "A Real Prince." *The Hollywood Reporter: Fresh Prince of Bel Air Salute,* September 16, 1994: S4.

———. "Will Smith." *The Hollywood Reporter: Fresh Prince of Bel Air Salute,* September 16, 1994: S6.

———. "Cashing In." *The Hollywood Reporter: Martin 100th Episode Salute,* February 22, 1996: S11.

———. "Scene-Stealers" *The Hollywood Reporter: Martin 100th Episode Salute,* February 22, 1996: S13.

———. "Attitude TV." *The Hollywood Reporter: Martin 100th Episode Salute,* February 22, 1996: S3.

———. "Birth of a Network." *The Hollywood Reporter: Salute to Fox Broadcasting on its 10th Anniversary,* May 13, 1997: S3.

Sklar, Robert. *Prime Time America: Life On and Behind the Television Screen.* New York: Oxford University Press, 1980.

Smith, Beretta Eileen. *Shaded Lives: Objectification and Agency in the Television Representation of African American Women, 1980–94.* UCLA Dissertation, 1997.

Smith, Danyel. "Martin Lawrence." *Rolling Stone,* November 11, 1993: 20.

———. "Heads Ain't Ready for Queen Latifah's Next Move." *Vibe,* December 1996–January 1997: 99–102.

Smith, Dinitia. "Color Them Funny." *New York Magazine,* October 8, 1990: 30–35.

Smith, Valerie. *Self-Discovery and Authority in Afro-American Narrative.* Cambridge: Harvard University Press, 1987.

Snitow, Ann, Christine Stansell, and Sharon Thompson, eds. *Powers of Desire: The Politics of Sexuality.* New York: Monthly Review Press, 1983.

Spigel, Lynn. *Make Room for TV: Television and the Family Ideal in Postwar America.* Chicago: University of Chicago Press, 1992.

Steenland, Sally. *Unequal Picture: Black, Hispanic, Asian and Native American Characters on Television.* Washington, D.C.: National Commission on Working Women, 1989.

Stern, Christopher. "Small Investments Yield Big Benefits: Networks Use Minority Interest in Stations to Lock in Affiliations." *Broadcasting and Cable,* October 17, 1994: 26, 28.

Stuckey, Sterlin. *The Ideological Origins of Black Nationalism.* Boston: Beacon Press, 1972.

Tartikoff, Brandon, and Charles Leerhsen. *The Last Great Ride.* New York: Turtle Bay Books, 1992.

Tate, Greg. "Cult-Nats Meet Freaky-Deke: The Return of the Black Aesthetic." *Village Voice Literary Supplement,* December 1986: 5–8.

Taylor, Ella. *Prime-Time Families: Television Culture in Postwar America.* Berkeley: University of California Press, 1989.

Thomas, Laurie, and Barry R. Litman. "Fox Broadcasting Company, Why Now? An Economic Study of the Rise of the Fourth Broadcast Network." *Journal of Broadcasting and Electronic Media* 35, no. 2 (Spring 1991): 130–57.

Tobenkin, David. "Plotting WB-ification." *Broadcasting and Cable,* July 25, 1994: 15.

Tom, Ron. "Sinbad: TV Star Plays Father on New Sitcom; Says Black Men Can Be Positive Role Models." *Jet,* November 22, 1993: 56–58.

Toop, David. *The Rap Attack: African Jive to New York Hip Hop.* Boston: South End Press, 1984.

Trescott, Jacqueline. "Fifteen Years and Rising for BET's Star." *Emerge,* September 1995: 66–67.

Tulloch, John, and Manuel Alvarado. "Sendup: Authorship and Organization." In *Popular Fiction: Technology, Ideology, Production, Reading,* edited by Tony Bennett. London: Routledge, 1990.

Turner, Graeme. *Film as Social Practice: Studies In Culture and Communication,* New York: Routledge, 1988.

Turner, Patricia. *Ceramic Uncles and Celluloid Mammies: Black Images and Their Influence on Culture.* New York: Anchor Books, 1994.

TV Guide. "The Fresh Prince of Bel Air," November 10, 1990. Robert MacKenzie: 48.

Udovitch, Mim. "Veni, Video, Vici." *Village Voice,* September 11, 1990: 51.

Walker, Alice. *Meridian.* New York: Harcourt Brace Jovanovich, 1976.

———. *The Color Purple.* New York: Harcourt Brace Jovanovich, 1982.

———. *You Can't Keep a Good Woman Down: Stories.* New York: Harcourt Brace Jovanovich, 1981.

———. *In Search of Our Mothers' Gardens: Womanist Prose.* San Diego, Calif.: Harcourt, Brace Jovanovich, 1983.

———. *Living By the Word: Selected Writings, 1973–1987.* San Diego, Calif.: Harcourt, Brace Jovanovich, 1988.

———. *The Same River Twice: Honoring the Difficult: A Meditation on Life, Spirit, Art, and the Making of the Film The Color Purple, Ten Years Later.* New York: Scribner, 1996.

———. *Anything We Love Can Be Saved: A Writer's Activism.* New York: Random House, 1997.

Wallace, Michele. *Invisibility Blues: From Pop to Theory.* London: Verso, 1990.

Waters, Harry F., and Janet Huck. "TV's New Racial Hue." *Newsweek,* January 25, 1988: 52–54.

Waters, Harry F., and Charles Fleming. "Amusing Ourselves to Def: Martin Lawrence Does the 'Man-Woman Thing.'" *Newsweek,* February 15, 1993: 47.

Waterman, David, and August Grant. "Cable Television as an Aftermarket." *Journal of Broadcasting and Electronic Media* 35, no. 2 (Spring 1991): 179–88.

Watkins, Mel. *On the Real Side: Laughing, Lying, and Signifying.* New York: Simon and Schuster, 1994.

West, Cornel. "The Dilemma of the Black Intellectual." *Cultural Critique* 1 (Fall 1985): 109–24.

———. "Marxist Theory and the Specificity of Afro-American Oppression." In *Marxism and the Interpretation of Culture,* edited by Lawrence Grossberg and Cary Nelson.Urbana: University of Illinois Press, 1988.

———. *Prophetic Fragments.* Trenton, N.J.: Africa World Press, 1988.

———. "The New Cultural Politics of Difference." In *Out There: Marginalization and Contemporary Culture,* edited by Russell Ferguson et.al. Cambridge: MIT Press, 1990.

———. *Race Matters.* Boston: Beacon Press, 1993.

West, Don. "Preston Padden: Strategizing to Move Fox from Underdog to Head of the Pack." *Broadcasting and Cable,* October 17, 1994: 18–26.

West, Don, and Kim McAvoy. "Tribune, Fox, Minorities Push Ownership Envelope." *Broadcasting and Cable,* October 10, 1994: 6–7.

Wexman, Virginia Wright. "Returning From the Moon: Jackie Gleason, The Carnivalesque, and Television Comedy." *Journal of Film and Video* 42, no. 4 (Winter 1990): 20–32.

Whetstone, Muriel. "Malik Yoba: Television's Renaissance Man." *Ebony,* February 1996: 148–52.

White, Mimi. "What's the Difference? *Frank's Place* in Television." *Wide Angle* 13, nos. 3–4 (July–October 1991): 82–93.

Whitehead, Colson. "21 Chump Street." *Village Voice,* September 27, 1994: 50.

Whitelaw, Kevin. "Reporting Live: Fox Takes on CNN." *U.S. News and World Report,* October 7, 1996: 51.

Wilkerson, Isabel. "Black Life on TV: Realism or Stereotypes?" *New York Times,* Arts and Leisure section, August 15, 1993: 1.

Williams, Frank. "Lessons from the Street," *Los Angeles Times,* Calendar section, May 25, 1997: 6.

Williams, Raymond. *Television: Technology and Cultural Form.* Hanover, N.H.: University Press of New England, 1974.

Wilson, William Julius. *The Declining Significance of Race: Blacks and Changing American Institutions.* 2nd ed. Chicago: University of Chicago Press, 1980.

———. *The Truly Disadvantaged: The Inner City, the Underclass, and Public Policy.* Chicago: University of Chicago Press, 1987.

Wood, Joe. "Who Says a White Band Can't Play Rap? Cultural Consumption: From Elvis Presley to the Young Black Teenagers." *Village Voice,* Rock and Roll Quarterly, March 1991: 10–11.

———. "United Paramount TV Lines Up Black Sitcoms." *Wall Street Journal,* June 5, 1996: B1.

X, Malcolm. *The Autobiography of Malcolm X.* Epilogue by Alex Haley. New York: Ballantine Books, 1992, c1965.

Zoglin, Richard. "Fresh Prince of Bel Air." *Time,* September 17, 1990: 75.

———. "Fox's Growing Pains." *Time,* August 23, 1993: 66.

Zook, Kristal Brent. "Light Skinned'ded Naps." In *Making Face, Making Soul: Haciendo Caras: Creative and Critical Perspectives by Women of Color,* edited by Gloria Anzaldúa. San Francisco: Aunt Lute Books, 1990.

———. "A Trip Through the Lives of the Versatile Mr. Jones: *Listen Up.*" *Accent LA,* October 1990: 12–15.

———. "Culture Club: A Talk with Producers/Directors George Jackson and Doug McHenry." *Village Voice,* November 26, 1991: 72–73.

———. "Reconstructions of Nationalist Thought in Black Music and Culture." In *Rockin' the Boat: Mass Music and Mass Movements,* edited by Reebee Garofalo. Boston: South End Press, 1992.

———. "Gagbangers." *Village Voice,* April 26, 1994: 43.

———. "Blackout: Charles Dutton Talks About Fox's Great Black Purge of '94." *Village Voice,* June 28, 1994: 51–54.

———. "Dismantling *M.A.N.T.I.S.*" *L.A. Weekly,* September 2, 1994: 41–42.

———. "The Jading Game." *Village Voice,* October 11, 1994: 52.

———. "Space Rage: *Cosmic Slop* Tears into the Forbidden Zone." *L.A. Weekly,* November 11, 1994: 51.

———. "Test Patterns." *Village Voice,* January 10, 1995: 64.

———. "Warner Bruthas." *Village Voice,* January 17, 1995: 36–37.

———. "Serious in Seattle: *Under One Roof* Breaks Prime Time's Ban on Black Drama." *L.A. Weekly,* March 17, 1995: 39–40.

———. "Still Waiting: Movies About Black Women Continue to Need Some Breathing Lessons." *Village Voice,* May 21, 1996: 6.

———. "21st Century Foxx." *Vibe,* March 1998: 66–72.

Personal Interviews

Chris Albrecht, October 1995.

Debbie Allen, April 1997.

Garth Ancier, December 1994.

Kevin Arcadie, March 1997.

Sam Art-Williams, July 1997.

Walter Allen Bennett, July 1997.

Christina Booth, July 1997.

Kyle Bowser, October 1993.

Yvette Lee Bowser, December 1993 and September 1997.

Calvin Brown, Jr., June 1996.

Takashi Bufford, June 1997.
Reggie Bythewood, August 1995 and March 1997.
Silvia Cardenas, July 1997.
Thomas Carter, March 1995.
Natalie Chaidez, March 1997.
Harriet Dickey, August 1997.
Richard Dubin, December 1993.
Bill Duke, August 1995.
Charles Dutton, June 1994.
Bentley Kyle Evans, August 1997.
Susan Fales, July 1996.
Ralph Farquhar, January 1994 and June 1996
Jamie Foxx, December 1997.
Lee Kyle Gaither, various conversations 1994–98.
Nelson George, various conversations 1990–98.
Kelly Goode, February 1995.
Sandy Grushow, October 1993.
Reginald Hudlin, October 1994 and February 1997.
Warrington Hudlin, various conversations 1991–98.
Robert Illes, August 1997.
Eugene Jackson, November 1993.
Jesse Jackson, various conversations 1994–98.
Phyllis Tucker Vinson Jackson, March 1994.
Sharon Johnson, August 1997.
Quincy Jones, September 1994 and April 1997.
Arnie Kogen, June 1997.
Don Kurt, August 1995.
Kyra Keene, July 1997.
Eric Laneuville, June 1997.
Debra Langford, June 1995.
Stan Lathan, January 1994.
Judy McCreary, July 1997.
Kathleen McGee Anderson, August 1997.
Benny Medina, June 1991.
Vanessa Middleton, July 1997.
David Mills, August 1997.
Rose Catherine Pinkney, June 1998.
Tim Reid, June 1994.
Darice Rollins, July 1997.
Janine Sherman, July 1997.
Sinbad, March 1994 and June 1996.

Will Smith, September 1994.
Marc Sotkin, June 1997.
Winifred Hervey Stallworth, September 1994.
Alison Taylor, May 1994.
Robert Townsend, December 1994.
Pam Veasey, July 1997.
Chuck Vinson, various conversations 1994–96.
Damon Wayans, June 1997.
Keenen Ivory Wayans, June 1993 and September 1997.
Shawn Wayans, December 1994.
Shawn and Marlon Wayans, January 1998.
Ed Weinberger, July 1997.
Dick Wolf, July 1997.
Malik Yoba, August 1995.

Television Programs

A Different World, NBC, 1987–91.
Amen, NBC, 1986–91.
America's Most Wanted, Fox, 1988–present.
American Family, unaired pilot, 1996.
The Beverly Hillbillies, CBS, 1961–71.
Beverly Hills 90210, Fox, 1990–present.
The Bill Cosby Show, NBC, 1969–71.
Blendin', unaired pilot, 1998.
Captivity, Fox, forthcoming.
Color Adjustment, PBS, 1992.
The Cosby Mysteries, NBC, 1994–95.
The Cosby Show, NBC, 1984–92.
Def Comedy Jam, HBO, 1990–97.
The Dick Van Dyke Show, CBS, 1961–66.
Diff'rent Strokes, NBC, 1978–85 and ABC, 1985–86.
ER, NBC, 1994–present.
Family Matters, ABC, 1989–97 and CBS, 1997–98.
Feds, 1997, CBS.
Fortune Hunter, Fox, 1994.
Frank's Place, CBS, 1987–88.
The Fresh Prince of Bel Air, NBC, 1990–96.
Friends, NBC, 1994–present.
Frontline: Who's Afraid of Rupert Murdoch? PBS, 1995.
George, ABC, 1993–94.

Goode Behavior, UPN, 1996–97.
Happy Days, ABC, 1974–84.
Hardball, Fox, 1994.
Homeboys From Outer Space, UPN, 1996–97.
Home Improvement, ABC, 1991–present.
Homicide, NBC, 1993–present.
House of Buggin', Fox, 1995.
The Hughleys, ABC, forthcoming.
I Love Lucy, CBS, 1951–57.
In Living Color, Fox, 1990–94.
In the House, NBC, 1995 and UPN, 1996–98 and NBC, 1998.
The Jamie Foxx Show, WB, 1996–present.
The Jeffersons, CBS, 1975–85.
Julia, NBC, 1968–71.
Linc's, Showtime, 1998–present.
Living Large, unaired pilot, 1988.
Living Single, Fox, 1993–97.
Lush Life, WB, 1996.
Malcolm and Eddie, UPN, 1996–present.
M.A.N.T.I.S., Fox, 1994–95.
Married. . . . With Children, Fox, 1987–97.
Martin, Fox, 1992–97.
Martin Lawrence: One Night Stand, HBO, 1989.
The Mary Tyler Moore Show, CBS, 1970–77.
Me and the Boys, ABC, 1994–95.
Miami Undercover, syndicated, 1961.
Miami Vice, NBC, 1984–89.
Moesha, UPN, 1996–present.
New Attitude, ABC, 1990.
New York Undercover, Fox, 1994–98.
NYPD Blue, ABC, 1993–present.
On Our Own, ABC, 1994–95.
The Parent 'Hood, WB, 1995–present.
Pearl's Place to Play, unaired pilot, 1994.
Picket Fences, CBS, 1992–96.
Players, 1997–98, NBC.
Roc, Fox, 1991–94 and BET, 1994–95.
Roseanne, ABC, 1988–97.
Sanford and Son, NBC, 1972–77.
Saturday Night Live, NBC, 1975–present.
The Show, Fox, 1996.

The Simpsons, Fox, 1990–present.
The Sinbad Show, Fox, 1993–94.
Sister, Sister, ABC, 1994–95 and WB, 1995–present.
Snoops, CBS, 1989–90.
Soul Train, syndicated, 1971–present.
South Central, Fox, 1994.
Sparks, UPN, 1996–98.
The Steve Harvey Show, ABC, 1995–96 and WB, 1996–present.
Sweet Justice, NBC, 1994–95.
Townsend Television, Fox, 1993.
The Wayans Brothers, WB, 1995–present.
Webster, ABC, 1983–87.
Wild Oats, Fox, 1994.
Working Guy, unaired pilot, 1996.
227, NBC, 1985–90.
413 Hope Street, Fox, 1997–98.

Films

Bad Boys, Michael Bay (director), 1995.
Boomerang, Reginald Hudlin, 1992.
Boyz N the Hood, John Singleton, 1991.
Car Wash, Michael Schultz, 1976.
Clockers, Spike Lee, 1995.
Crooklyn, Spike Lee, 1994.
Do the Right Thing, Spike Lee, 1989.
Fatal Attraction, Adrian Lyne, 1987.
4 Little Girls, Spike Lee, 1997.
Get On The Bus, Spike Lee, 1996.
Girl 6, Spike Lee, 1996.
Higher Learning, John Singleton, 1995.
Hollywood Shuffle, Robert Townsend, 1987.
House Party, Reginald Hudlin, 1990.
House Party 2, Doug McHenry, 1991.
House Party 3, Eric Meza, 1994.
I Like It Like That, Darnell Martin, 1994.
I'm Gonna Git You Sucka, Keenen Ivory Wayans, 1988.
Jungle Fever, Spike Lee, 1991.
Krush Groove, Michael Schultz, 1985.
Listen Up: The Lives of Quincy Jones, Ellen Weissbrod, 1990.
Malcolm X, Spike Lee, 1992.

Menace II Society, Allen and Albert Hughes, 1993.
Mo' Better Blues, Spike Lee, 1990.
Nothing to Lose, Steve Oedekerk, 1997.
Poetic Justice, John Singleton, 1993.
Rosewood, John Singleton, 1997.
School Daze, Spike Lee, 1988.
Set It Off, F. Gary Gray, 1996.
She's Gotta Have It, Spike Lee, 1986.
South Central, Steve Anderson, 1992.
A Thin Line Between Love and Hate, Martin Lawrence, 1996.
Waiting to Exhale, Forest Whitaker, 1995.
You So Crazy, Thomas Schlamme, 1994.

Music Recordings

Boogie Down Productions. *Criminal Minded.* 1985.
———. *By All Means Necessary.* 1987.
The Commodores. "Brick House." 1977.
En Vogue. "Theme from *Roc.*" 1993.
Aretha Franklin. "R.E.S.P.E.C.T." 1967.
The Fresh Prince and D.J. Jazzy Jeff. "Parents Just Don't Understand." 1988.
———. "Theme from *The Fresh Prince of Bel Air.*" 1990.
Grandmaster Flash and the Furious Five. "The Message." 1982.
N.W.A. *Straight Outta Compton.* 1988.
———. *Niggaz4Life.* 1991.
The O'Jays. "Family Reunion." 1975.
Dolly Parton. "Coat of Many Colors." 1969.
The Persuaders. "It's a Thin Line Between Love and Hate." 1971.
The Persuasions. "God Bless the Child." (Sung as theme from *Roc.*) 1991.
Public Enemy. *It Takes a Nation of Millions to Hold Us Back.* 1988.
———. "Fight the Power." 1989.
Queen Latifah, "Ladies First." 1989.
———. "Order in the Court." 1998
———. "U.N.I.T.Y." 1994.
Sly and the Family Stone. "Family Affair." 1971.
Tupac Shakur. "Dear Mama." 1995
Vanilla Ice, "Ice Ice Baby." 1990.

Index